The Rape of Sophia Perennis

Thank you for reading my book,

I hope you will thank me for writing it.

Cover design and artwork by the author

AuthorHouse™
1663 Liberty Drive
Bloomington, IN 47403
www.authorhouse.com
Phone: 1-800-839-8640

First published by AuthorHouse 8/18/2009

ISBN: 978-1-4389-7614-3 (sc)
ISBN: 978-1-4389-7615-0 (e)

Library of Congress Control Number: 2009907689

Printed in the United States of America
Bloomington, Indiana

This book is printed on acid-free paper.

Acknowledgments

When the writing of this book was nearing the end, the excitement began to build and for more than six months before the manuscript was submitted for publication, I sent copies to family and friends, and friends of friends, anyone I thought might be at all interested in reading it. I knew full well that this is not a book for every reader, and that many who received copies would find no satisfaction in reading the book, and would not likely finish it. In all fairness, early copies that were sent out were rough drafts, and polishing of the manuscript continued for another nine months until a few hours before it was submitted. To those who did provide feedback and encouragement I am grateful.

To Daniel Giamario, who supported the book by contributing knowledge gleaned from 39 years experience as a shamanic astrologer; thank you again for your support and all your help with tying astrology in with the 2012/shift theme of the last chapter.

To my long time friend John Bohn, who once said to me that there are no such things as ex-Catholics or ex-Marines. You can always be counted on for honest criticism, and I thank you for finding so little to criticize. I know that reading this book was painful for you, because you told me so, but you read it anyway. Thank you for your perseverance, and yes, I know I owe you for this.

To David Banner, academic mentor and advisor, who has traveled the world as a teacher and is himself a fine author; thank you for taking the time to read my book, for your suggestions and guidance, and for your glowing endorsement of my work.

To Ian Dixon, who has helped so many in so many ways with his services as a spiritual and intuitive counselor, psychic, and medium; thank you for the influence of your positive energy, for your support, your suggestions, and your enthusiastic endorsement.

Thank you to all who have seen this shift coming and blazed the trail that lay before us, who have set us on the path of seeking truth, and inspired seekers to become finders. Thank you to those who provided permissions to share their words in this book. Thank you especially to

Gregg Braden who took the time to talk with this first-time author, sharing ideas that helped work out important details in the last chapter of this book.

Most of all, to my wife, Michelle, who has shared with me, from start to finish, this sometimes excruciating experience; thank you seems so inadequate. In the last weeks before the manuscript was submitted, you were there to offer fresh perspectives and give me new views to consider. I'm sure that your eye opening perspectives have made this a better book. Thank you for being the best part of my life.

The Rape of Sophia Perennis

by

Garrison Edwards

Table of Contents

Introductions

Polarities

Processes

Oneness

Conclusion

*"People say they love truth,
but in reality they want to believe
that which they love is true."*

Robert J. Ringer

Preface

The introductions to Sophia Perennis and your author will be the subjects of chapters one and two, respectively. In this Preface, the book itself will be our topic. At about two hundred pages, this is not what one would call a large book, but as you read on you will discover that it discusses some very big ideas.

Let me begin by saying that this book is about truth. It discusses ideas that are essential to the way we see our world and our place in that world. Some of the ideas we will talk about are assumptions that have been handed down through generations, and form the foundations, the structure, of reality, as we know it.

As children, we learn how to use these ideas to construct an existence that fits within social expectations and the confines of consensus reality. Once we learn to adapt to this limited perspective on life, because these ideas so clearly express our experience of the world, we accept them as being true, and in the context of the reality we have constructed, they are true. These are relative truths, however, that may be true from one perspective and not necessarily from another. Though we will certainly discuss relative truth extensively, this book is *not* about that kind of truth. This book relates to relative ideas about truth as kind of a debunker, challenging the value of relative truth to the spiritual seeker.

1

The book is also about the nature of the higher reality that we seek; relief from all suffering in what many have called *the peace that surpasses all understanding*. See, there's one big idea we've introduced already.

The Ego

This is a word with many meanings, the most common of which are derogatory and relate to ideas like self-centered, self-serving, and self-aggrandizing. In psychology the term usually refers to the Freudian concept of the mental identity that emerges between the Id, which consists of drives or what might be called natural tendencies, and the Superego, which is the influence of our family and culture. There will be much talk of the ego in the coming chapters, and in this book the word ego will refer most directly to this psychological identity, and while the term egotistical is derivative of the Freudian meaning, what we will be talking about is this identity that is created in the mind. In the context of this book, consider the ego to be the mind created identity that we believe ourselves to be.

The Path

A path is a route leading from point A to point B, but when there is nowhere to go, a path becomes a useless concept. Understand this: there is no spiritual journey, you are exactly where you are supposed to be, and the only problem is that your ego wants to be somewhere else. Therefore, there is no teaching offered on these pages. The idea of a teaching means that there is something to be taught, information to be conveyed, or wisdom to be imparted. You already have everything you need. You will find a few statements of truth here, but no maps, no instructions, and no promises, just another finger pointing toward the moon.

The Premises

One of the aims of this book is to call into question some of our assumptions about truth by introducing compelling ideas that are alternatives to the views of popular opinion, authority, tradition, and in particular, religion. These alternative perspectives are valid in their own right and context, and they come from a variety of sources. In this book, I will quote scientists, philosophers, clergy, saints, sages, and more. I hope to assemble these disparate views into a mosaic that will reveal a perception of reality on a much grander scale.

In exploring these alternative ideas, we will question many of our preconceived notions about the world and perhaps discover the arbitrary nature of the parameters we set on reality. In the book, we will examine several polarities, such as "good and evil." We will talk about the processes of growing up and becoming a person, seeking truth, and the nature of time. We will consider unity or oneness as the fundamental reality, and we will talk about spiritual awakening as best we can. It is my intention to show that we hold a view of the world that is based on several minor misconceptions, all of which are based on one really big one. Let us not, however, get ahead of ourselves.

Another purpose of this book is to show evidence of a growing number of intelligent people who believe that our species and the entire planet are changing, evolving, expanding, not just in the physical sense, but also as consciousness and what might be called spirit. What we have been dealing with since the beginning of the twentieth century is something like a surge of evolutionary or spiritual energy, and life seems to keep going faster and faster.

In the final chapter we will talk about how the evolution of new species (if you believe in that sort of thing) happens in spurts, followed by long periods of stability. What I, and others, are seeing at this time in history seems to be such a surge, and it is much more than pushing the limits of what we can become – it is redefining what it means to be human.

Plain Talk

As this book is very concerned with issues surrounding religion in general and Western theology in particular, there is a danger of getting caught up in language and semantics, especially in a nonacademic book that does not allow space for lengthy explanations. A prominent feature of many spiritual teachings is jargon, or the use of terms that are exclusive to a specific teaching, or perhaps a language associated with a teaching, such as Hebrew, Latin, Arabic, or Sanskrit. Using terms like these can make these teachings seem more exclusive, mysterious, and thereby, attractive to the ego, but this use of *insider-speak* also sets up barriers that separate the believers from the nonbelievers.

Some of these insider-speak terms describe details of very complex ideologies, and complex ideologies are not always completely contained by our understanding of these insider-speak terms. When the mind learns a term for something, it believes it understands that something, when in fact, it may only understand the word. Equally subject to misunderstanding are terms like enlightenment, which stands for the ultimate simplicity, and which the mind will inevitably attempt to over-complicate.

For the sake of clarity, I have tried to avoid using insider-speak terms that have not been fully integrated into modern US English. When there are no other words to easily explain an idea, I will define any unusual or foreign words in the context that I use them.

Notes on Style

What I have attempted to do here is approach a wide audience by writing a simple but intelligent book while avoiding pretension. I come from humble roots and feel neither qualified to be, nor inclined toward being, pretentious. What I may be, occasionally, is irreverent. I find it difficult not to be irreverent when attempting to discuss some of this material in a rational fashion. Humor seems to me an essential ingredient in preventing dogma from degenerating into destruction. Therefore, I have injected small amounts of humor wherever I found appropriate.

This is neither a compilation nor a work of academic research, so I have chosen to use a bibliography and reading list rather than making specific references in the text. The first mention of a deceased historical figure or author will include a lifespan notation for perspective. As to dating I will use the currently accepted designations Current Era (CE) and Before Current Era (BCE) rather than Anno Domini (AD) and Before Christ (BC). Assume dates not indicated as BCE to be Current Era.

Future Works

This book was inspired and writing it interrupted two other works in progress. The working title of the first of these is *On Seeking*, and is an assessment of the primary tools that contribute to our understanding of our world and are used in our search for truth. These tools are science, the social sciences, philosophy, religion, and teachings that we call New Age. The second book is a spiritual autobiography with the working title *On Finding*. A third title, *On Being*, which is not yet begun, will complete a trilogy.

*"He who knows others is wise.
He who knows himself is enlightened."*

Tao Te Ching

Introductions

*"The Valley Spirit never dies.
It is called the Mysterious Female.
And the doorway of the Mysterious Female
is the base from which Heaven and Earth spring.
It is there within us all the time.
Draw upon it as you will, it never runs dry."*

Lao Tzu

Chapter One

Meet Sophia Perennis

Notwithstanding the provocative title, this book is not about a woman or an act of sexual aggression. Sophia Perennis is a Latin term that translates into English as "wisdom perennial." Please forgive the occasional anthropomorphic references to Sophia used throughout this book, I offer these references to the reader who may desire an image, a symbol, perhaps a mnemonic device, to associate with the real meaning of the term.

Sophia Perennis is also known as the eternal wisdom, perennial philosophy, and by other names that directly refer to ideas and teachings that focus on the universal underlying perspective that the nature of reality in general, and humanity specifically, is inherently divine. Sophia Perennis has been called the common transcendent core of all that we identify as religion. When an open mind grasps the principles of this eternal wisdom, the character of reality changes in an instant and the search for truth is finished. When one attempts to teach this wisdom, there are many opportunities for confusion. When Sophia Perennis is used to control or harm others, she is violated by those who claim to know and love her; and that is the rape to which the title of this book refers.

Many have written or spoken of Sophia Perennis, but relatively few have known her well. It is a rare occasion that she is seen clearly as she seems to operate at a different frequency from the judging mind; but she is always there, pointing not to the content of our awareness, but to awareness itself. When she manifests in our world she is usually either worshiped or persecuted, often both. In any case, she is almost certainly, to some degree, misunderstood; if not by the person she touched, surely words will fail to convey to others the depth and significance of the experience.

The Traditionalists

If you search the Internet for Sophia Perennis, two names that will come up are René Guénon (1886–1951) and Frithjof Schuon (1907–1998). French born René Guénon studied and taught metaphysics as it applies to cultural traditions, and though he has been called a philosopher, he preferred the title "exposer of traditional data." Raised as a Roman Catholic, he was not fulfilled by Catholicism and when he was 26, Guénon was secretly initiated into the Sufi Muslims and took on the Muslim name Shaykh `Abd al-Wahid Yahya. In 1920, he began writing prolifically in his native French emphasizing the non-spiritual nature of most religious teachings. One of his most avid followers was Swiss born religious scholar Frithjof Schuon who wrote dozens of books and has been published in a wide range of prestigious philosophical journals around the world. His work is highly respected by both academic and spiritual authorities.

Guénon and Schuon, along with a few others, are considered the founders of a philosophical movement, known as the Traditionalist School, which promotes the idea of Sophia Perennis as a way of interpreting traditional religious teachings in a mystical context. Like Guénon, Schuon, too, became a Sufi and as other philosophers joined the Traditionalists fold, most followed suit and converted to Sufism as well. On the Sophia-perennis.com website an article titled *What is Sophia Perennis; According to Frithjof Schuon* has this to say, "Strictly speaking, there is but one sole philosophy, the *Sophia Perennis*; it is also - envisaged in its integrality - the only religion."

Where is Sophia?

Despite the efforts of the Traditionalists, the eternal wisdom is not something that can be completely or concisely recorded in any specific philosophy or religion. As they will point out, however, her influence is ubiquitous, and once you know what to look for, this wisdom can easily be seen in Buddhist, Hindu and Taoist belief systems as well as in the mystery schools of Western religions. Eternal wisdom is less obvious in the more popular versions of Judaism, Christianity and Islam, which emphasize the salvation of the individual after death, over living in union with the Divine.

Sophia points toward an understanding that goes beyond the individual perspective to the foundations of everything that exists. Even though this ground of all being is expressed by the simplest of truths, these truths are non-conceptual and cannot be expressed clearly using language, and therein lies much of the problem. To say that Sophia's wisdom is beyond all concepts is meaningless to the mind because integrating concepts is primarily what the mind does. It translates our various perceptions into conceptual understanding so that knowledge can be structured and relationally integrated. Because it is the nature of mind to do so, it tries to impose that understanding by conceptualizing eternal wisdom as well. In the mind's world of concepts the ultimate truth is incomprehensible, and cannot be spoken of as we would speak of Earthly experience or knowledge. In his landmark book, *The Perennial Philosophy*, Aldous Huxley (1894–1963) had these comments, "The subject matter of the Perennial Philosophy is the nature of eternal spiritual Reality; but the language in which it must be formulated was developed for the purpose of dealing with phenomena in time. That is why, in all these formulations, we find an element of paradox. The nature of Truth-the-Fact cannot be described by means of verbal symbols that do not adequately correspond to it. At best it can be hinted at in terms of *non sequiturs* and contradictions." The teachings of Zen Buddhism abound with paradox, non sequiturs, and contradictions.

Zen makes no claims to truth and does not endeavor to teach eternal wisdom; rather, it attempts to open the aspirant to recognize the eternal in the present. Zen masters portray their teaching not as truth per se but as a finger pointing toward the moon. They recommend looking where the finger points rather than focusing on the pointing finger. The goal of Zen and most Eastern teachings is variously called awakening, enlightenment, moksha, nirvana, or Self-realization, wherein the sense of being an individual in a world of individuals becomes transparent so that the ever-present Oneness with the Divine is realized. In Western terms, this would equate to Christ Consciousness. It was Jesus (5 BCE–30 CE) who said, "I and the Father are One."

The Scene of the Crime

Western religions, as widely practiced, while based in similar principles, do not encourage seeking divinity in this world, but as a reward for compliance with their ethical teachings, offer eternal life as a separate individual in the company of the Divine. Based on a promise of heaven and the threat of hell, members of these religions learn to ignore the moon and hold in the highest regard the pointing finger of their particular religious writings, for each of these scriptures has been self-defined as the inerrant Word of God. This particular belief is near the root of the matter at hand; therefore, much of our attention will focus on the scriptures and doctrines of the three mainstream Western religions.

The doctrinal issues of Judaism, Christianity, and Islam vary widely even amongst the different sects of each major path. What ties them together beyond their Semitic origin is that they all believe in one God, who is the only true God, and are all based on faith, but faith in what? Beyond the fact that there are three (more or less) different sets of scripture, each claiming to be the only one that is true, there are a number of other good reasons why we need to exercise great caution in referencing ancient scriptures to help us understand Sophia.

First and foremost, as Huxley pointed out, any attempt to describe Sophia using language will tend to confuse most people, as Sophia does not fit well into any conceptual category; thus we have already gone astray at the first turn in the path. In addition, these scriptures were all canonized centuries before the invention of movable type; meaning that all translations and copies were made by hand, one letter at a time. We must also keep in mind that in Western theology, complex ideologies have been built around a few very simple ideas, and the connections between the ideology and the original teachings are not always obvious or logical. Stipulations of behavior, dress, and thought are spelled out repeatedly and in some detail in many of the major works of Western scripture. This makes them largely, if not primarily, social and ethical teachings as opposed to being purely spiritual.

Originally, the ideas of the founders of these religions may have pointed to truth, but these truths were conceptualized, taught to others, discussed, written down, copied, modified, and translated from language to language for centuries by flawed human beings who were entangled in culturally bound environments that have passed into antiquity, using languages that are inherently incapable of expressing the experience.

An Historical Perspective on Christianity

Prior to its acceptance by Constantine I (275–337) as the official religion of the Roman Empire, Christianity was little more than disorganized bands of rebellious Jews and a few gentiles with widely varying interpretations of the new approach that Jesus taught. One might prefer to assume that Constantine's conversion was due to some sort of spiritual awakening or a concern for the salvation of his soul or the souls of his subjects, but we should remember that Constantine was a politician and Emperor of Rome, and the overall welfare of the empire was his primary concern. Keep in mind also that Constantine himself was not baptized until he was on his deathbed. Consider perhaps that Constantine's motive might not have been purely spiritual and just may have been part of a well thought out plan to accomplish some political objective.

Regardless of the motivations behind Constantine's declaration, in 325, Christianity became the official religion of the Roman Empire, and if this new religion was to align itself successfully with the "powers that be" it would need to deploy a specific set of rules or laws to help Rome control the populace. Nearly three hundred years after Jesus died, influential representatives of the various Christian groups met and selected from the writings that were available at the time, what would become the Christian Canon. What we know as the Christian *Bible*, or *New Testament*, first came into existence in this way; but this is hardly the final version.

Popular Christian teachings include the teachings of Jesus, of course, but they emphasize the ideas of sin and salvation, making the sacrifice of Jesus more important than his teachings. While Jesus taught that the Kingdom of God is within, the foundational concepts of sin and salvation came from writings attributed to Paul (died c. 66), and were later refined by Saint Augustine (354–430). This emphasis is clearly evident in the New Testament Gospels which tell multiple versions of the miraculous birth of Jesus, take a brief look at his ministry, then jump almost immediately to the details of the last few days of his life.

Sin and salvation were essential to the early church, for catering to these aspects of the human condition placed the Church in a position of great power. The Church could now dictate the behaviors that would allow people to get to heaven, or for the disobedient, to hell.

Criticism from Within

In the last century, a new science has come into existence called textual criticism that looks at old manuscripts to determine their authenticity. When applied to religious documents it examines the history and development of the scriptures, primarily during the period before Guttenberg introduced movable type to the European continent.

Christian scholar and textual critic, Bart Ehrman had a "born-again" experience as a teenager and dedicated his life to God and Christianity. After high school, he majored in Bible Theology at Moody Bible Institute and went on to earn his doctorate in religious studies from the prestigious Princeton Theological Seminary. In his bestselling book *Misquoting Jesus; The Story Behind Who Changed the Bible and Why*, he tells us for what reasons and just how extensively the texts that compose what Christians call the *New Testament* have changed over time.

More often than not, the changes simply appeared to be errors; a letter misread, a line skipped, or a translation error. A significant number of cases, however, seemed to be intentional changes designed to alter the meaning of the text. Efforts to improve either the clarity or consistency of the book, to bring it into harmony with current interpretations, or to include a personal prejudice, were some of the suspected motivations for intentional changes.

Using all the material available to current scholars, the most conservative estimates indicate upwards of 200,000 variations between the oldest and most original texts available and the Bibles currently used today, while some authorities claim more than double that number. Ehrman concludes that, "There are more variations among our manuscripts than there are words in the New Testament."

Bart Ehrman followed his bliss down a road that he thought would bolster his beliefs; instead, it presented an objective view of his religion, which cast doubt on its veracity. The path of Dr. Ehrman's education and work analyzing Biblical scripture has depleted his faith from born-again, to mainstream Christian, to agnostic.

Yet here in the twenty-first century much of the population of the "civilized" world still claims to believe doctrines and propositions that are based on questionable documentation that was canonized and frozen in time to the education level, social standards, and ethics, of a culture that died out hundreds of years ago. As we certainly would not trust our health and welfare to their medicine and politics, why on earth would we invest our spirituality in their religion?

Fundamentalism

When you are a true believer, the Word of God is all you need, and justification in logic or reason is neither required nor desired. I remember a little song from Sunday school that I sang as a child, "Jesus loves me this I know, for the Bible tells me so." I wondered why, just because something is written in the Bible, we think that it must be true; but to the people who were charged with guiding me through the experience of childhood, the Bible was the Word of God. Though my family does not represent the hard core of the group, I would consider their view basically fundamentalist, which is concisely expressed by a popular bumper sticker that reads, "God wrote it. I believe it. That settles it."

On the subject of this very bumper sticker, Paul Alan Laughlin, an ordained Christian minister and former Chair of the Department of Religion and Philosophy at Otterbein College, in Ohio, writes in his book *Remedial Christianity: What Every Believer Should Know about the Faith, but Probably Doesn't*, "That really does not settle it, of course, for there are insurmountable problems with this viewpoint." Laughlin points out that the fundamentalist perspective that the Bible is inspired by God is not very convincing in light of the textual differences and versions of the documents composing the Bible, stating that "it is simply impossible to determine which, if any, of the many manuscripts of the various books might be the one thus inspired. Beyond this problem is the obvious variety of viewpoints (including theologies) in the Bible, as well as the undeniable contradictions at the factual level." Reading the Bible as literal also requires that one live, to some extent, in an ancient world where current scientific understanding is either wrong or not applicable. Laughlin adds that "Finally, it is difficult if not impossible to find a Fundamentalist who is literalistic about all parts of the Bible." In his book he points out that Christian Fundamentalists tend to worship on Sunday rather than the original Jewish Sabbath. They also allow women much more latitude than prescribed in the Old Testament. Unlike today, adultery and homosexuality were capital crimes in the early days of Western religion. He concludes with, "Fundamentalists generally tend to be literalistic about what *they choose* to consider 'fundamental' to the faith – which usually appears to be whatever censures beliefs and behaviors of which they disapprove." One may be inclined to ask, is it reasonable in our modern world to believe that the Bible is the inerrant Word if God? A literal interpretation of Christianity or any traditional religion will be at odds with what we know of the world. The scriptures are internally inconsistent, not believable as history, and considering the current state of affairs in the world, have not proven very effective at solving the problems of humanity.

And Now a Word from the Mystics

Within each of the major Western religions, however, there are sects that take a more mystical view of the teachings. There is, for example, the Sufi teaching within Islam and the Kabbalah of the Jewish religion. Laughlin suggests a few Christian alternative approaches to consider as well. "Pre-Christian Gnosticism had taught that the world was not created by a personal transcendent God, but emanated from an impersonal God, like light from a flame....Humans housed, or rather, imprisoned this Light-deity in their material bodies, which meant that the emanating God was immanent in them....Salvation was thus seen as the liberation of these spirits for their journey back to their Source."

Because of the literal interpretation of the term Gnosticism, it is often associated with knowledge, but as Laughlin points out, this is not knowledge in the usual worldly sense but might better be thought of as spiritual understanding or wisdom. These ideas were among the many contributing influences that shaped early Christian theology, and Christian Gnostics were legitimate Christians prior to 325 and Constantine. Laughlin describes the Gnostic view of Christ, "These Gnostic Christians taught that Jesus was...a teacher who had pointed to his own inner divinity in order to enlighten people about theirs."

Eventually falling out of favor with the mainstream church, it was determined that Gnosticism was in conflict with the accepted doctrine of Jesus dying on the cross for our sins, therefore, it was banned as heresy. The suppression of Gnosticism included the destruction of extensive writings, but in the mid twentieth century, two major finds revealed many previously unknown documents. Many were Christian Gnostic documents and are among the oldest original scriptures we have, and they point in an entirely different direction than does mainstream Christianity. Some non-canonical Christian documents, such as *The Gospel of Thomas* and a reconstructed gospel called *Q*, have been translated and published as books that anyone can buy.

Laughlin also offers Eastern Orthodoxy as an option to mainstream Christianity; "Eastern Christianity has never reflected the theological views of Paul and Augustine to the same degree as Roman Catholicism and Protestantism." In this view, humanity is not condemned from the start by original sin but is meant for perfection, "which could be achieved through the exercise of free will because of the divinization of humanity effected by the incarnation of Jesus." Other approaches that are mystical exist within the Christian based writings of Meister

Eckhart (1260–1327) or the teachings of Saint John of the Cross (1543–1591).

Laughlin makes it clear that, in his opinion, the traditional Western perspectives on monotheism (belief in one God) have not fared well historically and might better serve humanity when viewed mystically. Mystical monotheism translates roughly into monism (belief in nondual Oneness), which is the primary theology of the Far East, and at this point we are considering Hinduism, Buddhism, and Taoism. Laughlin seems to favor allowing Christians to consider other ways of viewing the religious experience, especially the monistic perspective. Laughlin so favors this approach to Christianity that he has written a second book, titled *Getting Oriented: What Every Christian Should Know about Eastern Religions, but Probably Doesn't*, which is designed to expose Christians to the mysticism of the East and to move toward, in his words, "an enlightened Christianity."

Summary

Religion that emphasizes individuality, either as the actions of free will, or as the salvation of the individual soul, focuses our attention on the smallest aspect of our being and moves us away from the wholeness of life that is the Absolute. Sophia becomes part of the picture when the desires of the individual ego become secondary to the larger reality of the One.

In Part II, Polarities, we will examine some familiar concepts in unfamiliar ways as we explore the boundaries of our self-limiting patterns of thinking. You may learn something you did not know before, but Sophia is not there. Sophia is not so much knowledge to be gained or a path to be followed, as it is submission to the eternal present moment.

Like life itself, Sophia exists only in the now, so do not look for her in the past or future, she is as close as your heartbeat or your current thought. But she is neither a thought nor a concept and is therefore invisible to the mind. Look for truth not in the world around you but in your own inner being, for your being *is* the eternal being that you seek. Sophia Perennis is the signpost along the spiritual path that leads you in the only direction you could possibly go; she is the existential cliff that beckons the seeker to embrace the eternal by disidentifying with the conditioned egoic personal self and awakening to the Oneness of *what is*. She is alive within each and every one of us as an impulse to move toward transcendence.

"What lies behind us and what lies before us
are tiny matters compared to what lies within us."

Ralph Waldo Emerson

Chapter Two

The Short Version of a Long Story

An interesting and potentially cathartic experiment that anyone can perform is to write an autobiography. It should be as long as you think it needs to be, and you may return to add memories when you recall them and new events as they occur. I started one about four years ago and it is growing sporadically. This exercise follows the dictum of Socrates (469–399 BCE) to "Know thyself." The other side of this Socratic wisdom reminds us that "The unexamined life is not worth living."

This book is about examining how we understand life in various ways; in this chapter, we will take a personal approach by telling a story. I do not know your story so I will tell the one that I would like to think I do know. An important part of this story is in the telling; it will become clear that while the story is told in first person, the perspective that dominates the narrative is that of an observer. You may use this convention when you write your own autobiography – or not; the effort really is about attempting an objective reevaluation of your most significant memories in determining what you believe you are. The following collage of verbal images represents to a small degree the life *I* have lived – *my* story.

Contraction into Identity

The previous sentence introduces a divisive attempt to draw attention to self-referent pronouns by placing them in italics. *I* will use this device only in this chapter, to remind the reader that the identity represented by words like *I*, *me,* and *my* is just an image. Because life requires that we do so, *I* learned to refer to *my* body, memories, feelings and thoughts; *I* learned to use these images, and their associated labels, to define who *I* am in this world. As we will soon find, the idea of a self requires that there be an *other*, which *I* will also place in italics – just in this chapter.

In the Beginning

This particular story begins in a small town in Ohio. Being raised in a more or less conventional Midwestern farm town makes it seem highly unlikely that a life would unfold in the ways that this one has. From earliest childhood, out of *my* perceptions grew an overwhelming sense of awe, there was wondering why and by what means this amazing world came to be. These thoughts took the form of memories and expectations, and they began to form an image of a perceiver with which the thoughts identified and held separate from what was being perceived. Generally speaking, *my* skin formed the boundary within which was contained the identity *me,* surrounded by *other*, which was *not me.*

The idea of an *other* became the compelling force in the creation and further definition of the *me* identity. *Other* manifested as people and things, the forces of nature, parental guidance and restrictions, and eventually, social conventions, religion, the law, and peer pressure. The *me* accumulated and incorporated thoughts and feelings as well as knowledge and physical possessions. *I* became increasingly aware of *my* body, mind, feelings, thoughts, toys, and in general, *my* relationship to everything that was *other*, but as with every child who is conditioned into an individual identity, what is aware of all this experience some-how slips into the background. It was the background that *I* wanted most to understand.

The Short Version of a Long Story

Based on what was becoming a highly refined memory structure, response patterns began to form that the *other* called *my* personality. These response patterns seemed to be both curious and skeptical, frequently challenging input that failed to integrate into the view of reality that was developing, especially if that information could not be verified or came from incredulous sources.

When *I* was about six, childhood encounters with nature started becoming an important influence on the way *my* process was developing. Adventures in the forest areas outside of town were the starting point for the development of a logic and reason filter that cross referenced and categorized *my* perceptions prior to validation. Many questions were arising and pat answers were unacceptable. *My* Christian heritage claimed to have all the solutions but the explanations offered would not pass through *my* logic and reason filter. *I* began looking elsewhere for answers. There will be more on *my* early struggles with Christianity in Chapter Eight.

I was only about eight years old when *I* came across a copy of *Siddhartha*, by Hermann Hesse (1877–1962). *I* was deeply impressed by this story of a brave young prince who left an enviable life of luxury behind to seek truth in the world and became The Buddha. This was my first meeting with the culture and philosophy of the Far East, but it would not be my last.

A couple of years later *I* read my first book by Alan Watts (1915–1973), *The Wisdom of Insecurity: A Message for an Age of Anxiety*. Though *I* cannot honestly say that *I* understood it, after all, *I* was only ten years old, there was something there that seemed extremely important and drew me in and made me want to understand. From Watts *I* learned about Zen and the societal taboo against knowing who you are. It was about this time that *I* started playing guitar and wrote *my* first song.

Around the age of eleven *I* developed an interest in Eastern martial arts, *my* practice, however, focused more on the meditative aspects than the combative. Though many of *my* rowdy friends liked to fight, and peer pressure made its demands, the trials of puberty would determine that *I* was a lover, not a fighter.

The Cruel War

I did not enjoy high school and got out the same year that "The Beatles" arrived in the US. The 60's counter culture began to erupt in the Western world and *I* was drawn in that direction. Music was becoming a powerful force, both in the culture at large and in *my* own life. At the same time the fighting in Vietnam escalated, and at the end of 1965, *I* received my draft notice to report for a pre-induction physical on the 27th of December. *I* successfully avoided the two year draft by enlisting in the Army for three years, but part of the deal was that *I* would be trained in the field of *my* choice. *I* chose personnel because I thought it would be a safe job if *I* was sent to the war. This turned out to be a very good idea since I was curious enough about the war to volunteer for duty in Vietnam. While in Vietnam, *I* became more involved with the martial arts, and reconnected with the writings of Watts and the ideas of Zen. *I* also turned twenty-one.

In the evenings *I* hung out with a few musicians and *other* imaginative people who were also stationed in base camp, and *I* organized a group of 15 or so creative people who would fly out in helicopters to secure field units and put on mini USO type shows to entertain the guys who were doing the actual fighting. In addition to being the organizer of the group, *I* played the role of "protest singer," strumming my guitar and singing songs like *Blowing in the Wind* by Bob Dylan and *Draft Dodger Rag* by Phil Ochs.

1968 was Quite a Year

I returned from Vietnam in March of 1968, and it had already been an eventful year. During January, *I* spent much of *my* time flying around entertaining the troops. Both the Company Commander and the Adjutant General endorsed *my* work in the field as an entertainer, but a new sergeant was assigned to supervise *my* work area and he didn't like the fact that *I* didn't do much work for him in the records department, where *I* was officially assigned. On January 31, the TET Offensive put an end to *my* activities as an entertainer, and *I* was now at the sergeant's disposal, so he "volunteered" *me* for every unpleasant duty he could find, everything from KP to going out and burying the burned bodies in a village that had been napalmed.

The Short Version of a Long Story

A friend who had a very good job as driver and personal aide to the Adjutant General was rotating "out of country" and with his recommendation, *I* was reassigned to his old job for the remainder of my tour. Just before leaving Vietnam for home, *I* went to Hong Kong for a week of R&R.

Upon returning to the States, *I* married the "girl back home," and moved to the East coast, which would be home for the last year of *my* enlistment. It was an interesting time to be in *my* position; a twenty-one year old Vietnam vet trying to serve out *my* time so *I* can establish a life in the real world. Meanwhile, *I* am fully aware that the world in which this life will be established is completely insane, and the events of the year 1968 made a strong case for that position.

North Korea seized the spy ship USS Pueblo and shot down a US spy plane. The big Vietcong TET offensive and the infamous My Lai massacre both happened before *I* left Vietnam. Opposition to the Vietnam War enabled Eugene McCarthy to run for president and caused Lyndon Johnson to announce that he would not run. Martin Luther King was killed in April, setting off race riots across the country. In May, nine Catholic priests were arrested for breaking into a Selective Service office and burning draft records. In June, Bobby Kennedy was assassinated. The Democratic Presidential Convention in Chicago turned into a riot. Saddam Hussein and Yasir Arafat became political figures in the Middle East. Apollo 7 spent eleven days in space. Harvard professor, Timothy Leary was prescribing LSD as the cure for all of the ills of humanity, and Richard Nixon was elected president. Yes indeed, 1968 was quite a year.

Changes

Upon release from the Army in the spring of 1969, not wanting to live too close to our families and their influence, we moved far enough away to make visiting inconvenient but not impossible. It was the dawn of a new era and there were basically three "lifestyle choices" that were available to us. The sellout route was to follow the road of history and enter the straight world that grew out of the influence of our parents and culture. As the dominant culture, contact with the straight world was, of course, inevitable, but the counterculture placed some options at the fringes of the Bell curve. The counterculture options were based on two somewhat radical perspectives; we found the "peace and love" policy of the hippies more attractive than the political activism of the yippies and their ilk. *I* took a job managing a small retail pet shop and the wife went to work as a beautician. *I* liked retailing, but after a year, the owners divorced and closed the shop. Local job searches came up empty, so *my* wife cleaned up *my* haircut, *I* went to an employment agency, and took a job in Chicago as an assistant manager for F. W. Woolworths.

The next year was a qualified disaster and we left Chicago with nowhere to go except back to the home of our families. These were lean times spiritually speaking; the way it felt was stuck and frustrated. Zen was no longer moving things forward in this search for truth that had become *my* life. *I* had enjoyed smoking pot since Vietnam but had no interest in the "harder" drugs. Perhaps it is ironic that after traveling halfway around the world, it was *my* high school friends, in the town where *I* was born and raised, who introduced *me* to the big league hallucinogens, LSD, peyote, and psilocybin. *I* took one or the other twenty to twenty-five times over the next few weeks; after about a month *I* was finished and never took anything like that again.

Eckankar

I was in my mid-twenties, a few years out of the Army, when something of a spiritual breakthrough occurred. *My* wife brought home a book by Brad Steiger, titled *In My Soul I Am Free*. It was about a man named Paul Twitchell who had founded a spiritual organization that he called Eckankar. In addition to being about Twitchell, the book outlined some basic principles of Eckankar. *My* wife and *I* both resonated with this teaching and sought out a local group of Eckists, which we joined.

I found Eckankar to be an aggregate of Eastern religions, explained clearly in everyday English. It was 1970, and the hippy movement of the 60's was beginning to mellow into the New Age. There was meditating, much like the style used in Zen, there was intellectual understanding available in the many Eckankar books, and there was a supportive environment of peaceful loving people that crossed economic, social, and age strata. There were powerful spiritual experiences of unity that began to open *me* up to the Oneness. It was all very nice and for seventeen years, this was *my* spiritual life, but a point came when the path took a turn and I did not follow. Still, *I* look back on those days as a good time; *I* wrote songs about the path and sang them at Eckankar gatherings and conventions around the country.

Turning a Page

Things were moving very quickly, and within a span of eighteen months a child was born, a marriage was dissolved, and there were two road-trips out West. At a large Eckankar gathering in October *I* sang my songs to a crowd of 15,000, and at a small seminar a month later, *I* met Michelle. Instantly, a bond was forged between us that would last a lifetime. Our relationship clearly was a fated thing, and eight months later we were married and living in Cleveland.

The leadership of Eckankar changed and *my* enthusiasm for the path started to wane. Though *I* remained a member for quite a while after that, *I* took the spiritual insights gained and returned to science, an old friend from childhood.

It was the late 1970's, when *my* wife, Michelle, who had her bachelor's degree, convinced *me* to give college a try. After a community college practice run, *I* entered the local university as a psychology major. About the same time *I* started investigating the ideas of quantum mechanics and relativity. The implications of these ideas were astounding, but they were failing to infiltrate mainstream thought. *I* had seen the similarities between Eastern mysticism and the "new physics" pointed out by the likes of Fritjof Capra and Gary Zukav, and *my* reason and logic filter did not reject their ideas. *I* enjoyed these books immensely and took some comfort in the possibility that, having been at odds for centuries, the science that structured *my* thinking and the spiritual foundations *I* was seeking, might ultimately hold a common view, or at least compatible views, of reality.

Crash on a Twisting Road

High school had been unfulfilling at best, but college went rather well. As an undergraduate *I* worked on department research as a data analyst, founded a student psychology club and a Chapter of Psi Chi, the National *Honor Society* in Psychology, and attended a postgraduate workshop with Lawrence Kohlberg at Harvard. Academic success was a new and delightful experience.

After the college experience, *I* took a sabbatical and tried sculpting. *I* developed a style and produced a small body of work. Marketing seemed in conflict with the creative part, and trying to do both was not working out. *My* wife had an idea for a software company and *I* offered to help. This was never intended to be a career, but it kind of turned out that way. Ten years later the company had grown up around us to become quite successful.

For several months *I* had been getting tired during the day, even taking naps at lunch, but thought *I* was just overworked like many Americans. The first real symptom was a simple itch that became pervasive, so *I* went to the doctor. His first thought was allergies, but he ordered blood work just in case. After a return to the lab for a second round of tests he called *me* into his office. He did a little verbal dance around the subject, then gave the "good news/bad news" delivery – "we're pretty sure that it isn't pancreatic cancer," he said, "but there seems to be a serious problem with your liver."

I went to a major clinic and eventually got the attention of the Head of Hepatology who started by treating "the itch." The itch, which is typically symptomatic of a wide range of liver problems, is not well understood, nor easily treated. It can be agonizing at times but is not a very useful diagnostic tool, therefore, he was reluctant to say precisely what was wrong with me. The itch, however, was no longer *my* only symptom; there was now severe lower back pain, and major muscle spasms in *my* back and legs. The back pain was caused by compression fractures, and was separate from the muscle spasms, but they were allies in creating the most excruciating pain of *my* life.

I began losing strength fast so the clinic sent *me* to a small private rehab hospital, where the pain lessened when *I* was given the highest dose of fentanyl available in a transdermal patch. Fentanyl is a highly addictive, extremely powerful synthetic opiate that is usually reserved for cases where nothing else works, such as terminal cancer patients.

The Short Version of a Long Story

Nothing else *had* worked so the clinic continued prescribing fentanyl. It was now several months into treatment and *I* did not yet have a diagnosis, so they did more tests and finally, this thing was given a name; primary biliary cirrhosis – stage four, the most advanced condition of this incurable, progressive, and debilitating disease. The clinic doctors recommended that *I* get on the liver transplant list as soon as possible.

About the age of twenty five, this body settled into a consistent configuration that was 6'0" tall and 150 lbs. I mention this because while investigating the source of the back pain the clinic discovered advanced osteoporosis. Lumbar compressions fractures had taken four inches of *my* height before *I* knew it was gone, and between vomiting several times a day from the fentanyl, and muscle atrophy from weakness, *I* lost 25 lbs. off an already slim body. When *I* look at pictures of "myself" from this period *I* am still stunned at how sick *I* was, and ever so thankful to be here to tell the story.

I was in bad shape when a wonderful book by Louise Hay, *You Can Heal Your Life*, explained that liver problems grow out of long held anger. *I* believed, after a brief self-examination, that, in *my* case, she was correct. *I* also believed that all physical illness is psycho-somatic, but Louise Hay had given me a map. When presented with an irritating circumstance, *I* simply ask the question, "Is this important enough to die for?" The answer was obvious, and if this liver problem turned out to be a mental thing, *I* was just the guy to fix it.

When *I* declined to go on the liver transplant list *my* doctors pretty much resigned themselves to keeping me comfortable rather than fighting the inevitable. They believed that without the liver transplant *I* didn't have long, and were not sure that *I* would even survive the transplant waiting list. Sharing their concern, *my* wife found the time and the funds (not sure where she got either) to take *me* to Disney World. *I* was in a wheelchair, of course, and this got us to the head of all the lines, which was nice. Overall, it was a good trip, and to the degree that it was possible, *my* spirits were lifted by the experience.

After we returned from Florida, *I* decided that relief from the pain was not worth what the fentanyl was doing to *me* The insurance plan did not cover drug detox, so it was up to *me* to get off the fentanyl. After two failed attempts at cold turkey the prescription was reduced over a few months from 100 µg per hour to 75, 50, and 25, at which point *I* figured out a way to divide the patches further and reduced the dosage until *I* was able to quit with relatively mild withdrawal.

When this illness began in the summer of 1998, our business had grown from a $3500 investment ten years before into a $5 million regional consulting services company. Moving into the new millennium, however, the business climate changed drastically and so did our world.

We spent seven months in South Carolina where both of us, in our own ways, began to heal. In June of 2003, we moved to Arizona, arriving one sunny afternoon to meet the 111 degree heat with a broken air conditioner. We've been here for a while now and life keeps getting better. *I* still meet with *my* doctors twice a year, and *I* still have the disease, as the annual sonogram continues to confirm cirrhosis. I've gained the weight back but not the height. The pain can usually be ignored without medication and *I* feel nearly *normal* these days, though normal has been redefined within the context of the situation.

When *I* first started feeling better just before leaving South Carolina, *I* had to do something, so *I* read a lot, and when able, wrote down *my* thoughts as sort of an electronic journal. *My* cognitive skills had been dulled by the pain medications and it was good to feel them returning. It soon became clear that the writing was a tool to reorganize and solidify a new life view. The writings began to take the form of a book with the working title *On Seeking*. *On Seeking*, which has been set aside until this book is finished, addressed in a very broad sense, the idea of seeking higher truth, and the nature of the writing required a great deal of reading to support and expand the ideas in that book.

The research, some of which is used in this book, was mostly academic but included a variety of spiritual teachings as well. *I* loved reading about the science, but the writings of the ancient philosophers and spiritual masters, like the teachings of Christianity, addressed the consciousness of a different culture in a different time. *I*, who had grown up in a small Midwestern farming community, had difficulty relating to translations of books originally written in ancient languages.

Opening the Gate

However, *I* also encountered many modern spiritual masters who have come from all walks of life, who live, in current times, lives that are both ordinary and extraordinary. There appears, in *my* view, to have been a surge of enlightened teachers over the last fifty to a hundred years and the numbers seem to be increasing. The general rise of world population may be partially responsible, as well as advances in communications, along with improvements in publishing brought about by computers and technologies such as print on demand, but *I* have recently observed a veritable avalanche of books on enlightenment along with a growing presence on the Internet. While there has been increased interest in traditional religious teachings as well, both Eastern and Western, what excites me most is the popularity of books by authors and teachers who offer paths that have no doctrine or dogma.

The End of Seeking

After decades as a spiritual seeker, the idea that *reality, as it is experienced, is an illusion*, had presented itself in various Eastern formats. The results of my cross validation process, however, were inconclusive; *I* believed but did not yet know. While poring over volumes of recent work in physics, medicine, social sciences, philosophy, and more, researching material for the first book, *I* began to receive flashes of the forces that hold reality together.

I began to see reality as energy in motion, shimmering and somewhat translucent, and then around the middle of August, 2003 everything changed forever. In an instant the mysteries of life became clear to the extent that for a few hours visual objects actually appeared transparent, and *I* moved carefully so as not to bump into things. The end came rather abruptly *I* thought, certainly not something one would anticipate or expect, hardly an experience at all in the usual sense. It was suddenly seeing something very obvious that was there all along; just unnoticed. It did not feel much like one might expect of an awakening, it was more like slapping yourself on the forehead when you finally "get" a really clever joke. It was as simple as that. Existence opened up and became a beautiful, pulsating, living, timeless, infinite, Oneness. *I* was in the universe while it was also in *me*, there was nothing and no one to be separate from.

I had no more questions of life, and *I* knew that the book *I* was writing was no longer being written primarily to reorganize the life view of the individual *me*, for that *me* was revealed to be but a character in a dream into which *I* had awakened. *I* knew something profound had occurred, but there were no words to describe it, and it was a few days before *I* even tried to share with *my* wife what had happened.

There was a new *me* that was aware of the individual's place in the universe, but no longer completely identified with that individual. The ego with which *I* had always identified was debunked, devalued, and yet amused by a sense of peace and awe that dissolved the resistance that usually accompanies duality. There were no words, but there was a welling up in *my* chest that erupted in a beaming smile punctuated by a little chuckle, and for about a week it seemed like *I* couldn't stop smiling.

The perspective of nonduality is that there is no self, and that what we perceive as our self is only the ego, and the ego, as we shall soon see, is merely an image created from a collection of thoughts. When the *I*, which had been so painstakingly constructed from the ideas, judgments, and experiences of a lifetime, recognized its illusory nature, it quietly stepped aside to reveal the simple non-conceptual truth that is the foundation of existence; there is only One. *My* experience of life is now analogous to a dream in which all the characters and other appearances emanate from the consciousness of One dreamer, and the dreamer is so much more than the *I*.

"There is neither creation nor destruction,
Neither destiny nor free-will;
Neither path nor achievement;
This is the final truth."

Ramana Maharshi

Polarities

*"In the gap between subject and object
lies the entire misery of humankind."*

Jiddu Krishnamurti

Chapter Three

Duality vs. Nonduality

Duality and nonduality are not words often heard in everyday conversation; if you are familiar with them at all you are likely thinking of Cartesian dualism, but that is not what is being considered here. Descartes (1596–1650) referred to the dualism of mind/body, but here we are addressing the more fundamental dualism of self/other. The perspective of dualism relies on the existence of an "other" in order to maintain a "self." The concept of a separate self requires that it be separate from something; therefore, if there is a self there will always be an "other." Other can be other individuals, groups, nature, the universe, God, the unknown, anything recognized as not self. Dualism is a perspective that separates, defines, judges and categorizes things and experience. It is the perspective of science and everyday life; it is based on observation and is justified by what we call "common sense." Dualism is the prevailing point of view in the Western world so I will respect your common sense by not dwelling on the obvious and move on to a perspective that might be less familiar. Before discussing nonduality, however, we must first understand that the truth of nonduality is not at all like the truth of duality.

The Concept of Nondual Truth

From the nondual point of view, the very idea of truth in duality is something of an oxymoron, and these written words before you are but another manifestation in that duality. Still, the mind will pull at the words to extract meaning, dividing every sentence into subject, object, and verb, because that is what the mind does. It is part of the normal learning process that when we encounter new ideas they must integrate into our current thought structure or they will likely be dismissed as either incorrect or irrelevant. I ask that you try to hold that urge at bay; nonduality does not fit well into any structure in the mind, but relates more to the space that allows those structures to exist. If one maintains an open mind, and pays attention, what we will be discussing in this chapter may aid the reader in understanding nonduality as an intellectual concept. In these times of spiritual expansion, many are gaining this intellectual understanding.

Understanding nonduality as a concept is to accept nonduality as the theoretical platform on which all reality rests. The nondual perspective says that the Absolute, by definition, is All That Is, and includes all apparent separations from that Oneness. David Loy, international authority on religion and ethics, begins the *Introduction* to his book, *Nonduality: A Study in Comparative Philosophy*, with a quote from Plotinus (205–270), whose ideas of Neo-Platonism became very popular and influential in the development of religious thought throughout early Western civilization. "There were not two; the beholder was one with the beheld; it was not a vision compassed but a unity apprehended." Loy continues in his own words to discuss nonduality in Western culture, "The nonduality of seer and seen: there is no philosophical or religious assertion more striking or more counterintuitive, and yet claims that there is such an experience, and that this experience is more veridical than our usual dualistic experience, are not rare in the Western tradition. Similar statements have been made, in equally stirring language, by such important Western mystical figures as Meister Eckhart, Jakob Boehme, and William Blake, to name only a few. Philosophers have generally been more hesitant about committing themselves so decisively, but a claim regarding the nonduality of subject and object is explicit or implicit

36

within such thinkers as Spinoza, Schelling, Hegal, Schopenhauer, Bergson, and Whitehead – again naming only a few."

Consider the case of Meister Eckhart, the German Christian mystic who was charged with heresy because he suggested ideas such as, "The knower and the known are one. Simple people imagine that they should see God as if he stood there and they here. This is not so. God and I, we are one in knowledge." Eckhart died before the heresy proceedings were complete, but two years after his death, twenty-eight of his statements of belief were condemned as heretical.

Offered as a philosophical example, Arthur Schopenhauer (1788–1860) understood nonduality in this way, "As an individual, with your death there will be an end of you. But your individuality is not your true and final being, indeed it is rather the mere expression of it; it is not the thing-in-itself but only the phenomenon presented in the form of time, and accordingly has both a beginning and an end. Your being in itself, on the contrary, knows neither time, nor beginning, nor end, nor the limits of a given individuality; hence no individuality can be without it, but it is there in each and all. So that, in the first sense, after death you become nothing; in the second, you are and remain everything."

Nonduality in Western Religion

Mainstream Western religions, while they originate from and accept mystical practice of the faith, do not usually encourage the pursuit of such ideas and keep them isolated from the general doctrine. While the Jewish and Islamic systems appear somewhat ambivalent to mystical sects within their ranks, throughout history Christianity has made a concerted, often violent, effort to squelch any signs of deviation from the doctrine as written and prescribed by the Church.

In current times, the rare, mystically inclined, Christians who seek the perspective of nonduality are called contemplatives. A follower of St. John of the Cross, Bernadette Roberts tells of her experience as a Christian contemplative in *The Path To No-Self: Life at the Center*. In the introduction to her book, she begins with the basics, "Traditionally the Christian contemplative life is divided into three states, or stages, of progress: purgative, illuminative, and unitive, with the last regarded as the definitive, most perfect attainment of the soul in this life." Roberts prefers to view the unitive state as another transitional stage, rather than as the end of the contemplative journey. She talks of the unitive state as the final stage of *selfhood*, where "holiness can be achieved because holiness belongs to the suffering self, a self able to give unceasingly without receiving in return – a life devoid of self-satisfaction." The end of the unitive stage takes the soul beyond the self, and at this point one's perspective will change. She explains, "Once beyond the self, however, holiness is no longer possible because now, there is nothing left to give and no one left to do the giving." A short but interesting excerpt of her writing can be found in another book, along with the words of other enlightened authors.

Nonduality in Other Areas

Jerry Katz has written, and compiled writings by Roberts and others into a book titled *One: Essential Writings on Nonduality*. Katz has been running the nonduality.com web site for some time and has, no doubt, been exposed to a great deal of information on the topic. He probably knows as much as anyone about the subject of nonduality. His book is a plethora of interesting data that will certainly stimulate most enquiring minds. It is presented in five parts, each of which approaches nonduality from a different direction. Part one of Katz's book attempts to answer the question, "What is Nonduality?" Part two is dedicated to a dialogue with the well known twentieth century Indian sage, Ramana Maharshi (1879–1950). In part three Katz shares stories told by representatives from mystical sects of the three Western religions, various Eastern teachings, and one account from a Native American tradition. In part four he presents specific examples of the application of nondual wisdom in the fields of psychotherapy, education, art, and the cinema, devoting a chapter to each application. In part four he quotes transpersonal psychologist and author, John J. Prendergast.

Prendergast began practicing Transcendental Meditation in 1970, and has studied under various nondual teachers including Ammachi, Jean Klein, and Adyashanti. He has taught a number of workshops for therapists including presentations at Conferences on Nondual Wisdom and Psychotherapy. Regarding the use of nondual wisdom in psychotherapy, Prendergast had this perspective to offer: "[An] impact of an awakening nondual awareness is an enhanced capacity to be with *what is*. All mainstream schools of psychotherapy understand the importance of acceptance, yet the dualistic mind can never be an agent of complete acceptance. The mind only accepts *what is* conditionally, hoping that if something is accepted, it will change. The living insight of nondual awareness is that everything already is accepted and embraced just as it is. As awakening deepens, the judging mind loses its grip and attention becomes increasingly innocent, intimate, and impersonally affectionate."

Part five of Katz's book consists of four short chapters that consider the question, "How can things appear so individualistic and be non-separate?" Questions such as this are of concern only because the dualistic mind struggles to comprehend reality in terms of concepts. When nonduality is fully realized, questions of this nature are no longer relevant and the seeking of spiritual truth in duality ends.

Beyond an intellectual understanding, to fully realize nonduality is to embody Oneness and become nondual, which is also called enlightenment or awakening. To awaken is to move attention from the dualistic perspective of the individual, into nonduality where the individual is an expression of Oneness.

Realizing the nondual nature of reality is to escape the fortress of mental energy that defines the self as the ego, where all that is known to the mind must be evaluated and measured, where opinions are required. Duality is a world created by the mind and in the words of Alan Watts, "When one speaks of awakening it means dehypnotization, coming to your senses; but, of course, to do that you have to go out of your mind." As you read this book, I ask you to remember that there is a vast schism between understanding nonduality as a mental concept, which can be quite difficult in itself, and realizing it as non-conceptual truth. I trust that most who have realized nonduality, at one time, believed they understood it. I also suspect that very few were not surprised at what they found when awakening occurred.

Nondual Traditions

If you find the idea of nonduality intriguing but prefer a traditional path, there are options available. I will not attempt to offer, in this small volume, anything beyond the briefest glimpse of these paths. As already mentioned, there are mystery schools relating to nonduality in the three major Western religions, but other nondual traditions exist in teachings of the Far East. Let me begin by saying that Hinduism, Taoism, and Buddhism all lean more toward nonduality than do the popular Western religions. This is not to imply that they are all the same, however, as there is a wide range of beliefs and structures involved.

Indian Hinduism, which some scholars have dated as far back as 1500 BCE, is a fully developed social structure in addition to a variety of theologies that differ widely in practice. Of the various Hindu teachings, the one that most directly approaches nonduality would be Advaita Vedanta. Most authorities believe that Adi Shankara (788–820) consolidated the doctrine of the Vedanta to form the Advaita School around the 9th century; he wrote, "Brahman is the only truth, the world is illusion, and there is ultimately no difference between Brahman and individual self." They are so closely integrated with the Indian culture that the Hindu religious teachings, until the last hundred years or so, have remained largely confined to the Indian subcontinent.

Joseph Campbell (1904–1987) called Buddhism, Hinduism packaged for export. Also out of India, Buddhism, which does not incorporate the social structures of Hinduism, developed later and has gone through one major split and many smaller ones as it quickly spread across Asia. Within the Buddhist religion, a highly streamlined path developed in China around the 6th century CE. Chan Buddhism, as it is called, teaches that enlightenment can occur without necessarily following the mental or physical disciplines laid out by the original Buddha. In practice, most forms of Buddhism involve rituals and reading of scripture much like Western religions. Chan, however, seeks enlightenment directly through meditation, contemplation, and the use of mentally challenging ideas in the form of short riddles called koans. Chan spread throughout Asia and was discovered by the West in Japan.

Zen is an Indo-European word based on the Japanese pronunciation of Chan, and that is how Zen became known in the West.

Some of the oldest and most powerful writings we have on nonduality are found in a small book of poetry called, *The Tao te Ching*, attributed to the Chinese sage Lao-Tzu (*c.* 6th century BCE), legendary founder of Taoism. *The Tao te Ching* confirms the ineffable quality of nondual truth by opening with the disclaimer that the Tao that can be spoken of is not the Eternal Tao. While Western religions have attempted to fit their nondual foundations into the context of Western culture, Taoism adapts the culture to work in a nondual framework. Taoism offers a wide variety of practices that deal with the spectrum of human activity from seeking enlightenment to healing problems with the physical body. The history of Tai Chi is strongly linked to Taoism, as is acupuncture.

Taoism promotes the ideal of an ego-less, self-less state, where the Tao or the *way of nature* is in charge of one's life; it emphasizes nonduality, interdependency, and a society that is free from desire. Taoism teaches no absolutes, ethics or dogma other than the practice of Wu Wei, which translates as non-action or effortless actions, performed without desire, that are in harmony with the Tao. Taoism points out that through desire we make judgments and conceptualize the notions of good and bad, and by clinging to these notions we cling to duality. The Taoist symbol of yin and yang depicts graphically the idea that opposites embrace and contain each other to define the whole. The whole is the good and bad, the righteous and evil, the source of all that is, the Absolute, the whole enchilada, without exclusion, exception or opposition; this is what Sophia Perennis calls God.

Modern Teachers

As mentioned earlier, there has been a veritable avalanche of nondual teachers in recent years and I feel fortunate to live in a time of such a worldwide surge of spiritual expansion. Presently, many authors and teachers are available to point the way. I have included at the end of this book, a list of authors for those who are sincerely seeking ultimate truth. Though their styles and specific approaches may vary, their words point to a pure awareness that supersedes any conceptual understanding of reality and are, in that sense, not easily grasped by the mind. Concepts, thoughts and perceptions are the content of awareness and will be understood in whatever way they are evaluated by the conditioned mind, but pure awareness exists, apart from any content, as the stage or the screen on which the drama of existence unfolds. Pure awareness is allowing and accepting, but it is not something you can attain as a possession or a state of consciousness; pure awareness is the power at the core of your being that makes reality possible. The Sophia Perennis that "I" have come to know is anything that points to this pure awareness as our true nature. Presented here, in alphabetical order are small offerings from a few of the modern nondual teachers who have influenced me most.

The first chapter closed with the thought that Sophia is, among other things, "an impulse to move toward transcendence." *The Impact of Awakening: Excerpts from the Teachings of Adyashanti* begins with a discussion of a similar idea as *The Evolutionary Impulse to Be Free.* "The impulse to be free is an evolutionary spark within consciousness which originates from beyond the ego. It is an impulse toward the divine, unity, and wholeness. It is an impulse originating from the Truth itself." This impulse has nothing to do with seeking to attain truth or anything else, but as the ego tries to understand this impulse, it is conceptualized and co-opted by the ego; it is this that creates the illusion of the spiritual seeker. The spiritual seeker is created when this impulse is interpreted by the ego as lack, a need to be fulfilled. The ego then seeks to fill that lack, that void, in the only way it knows how; by making itself stronger, braver, truer. Adyashanti goes on to describe awakening, "When you awaken, all becoming ceases. Being awake means that you realize by direct experience who and what you are. You do not become anything. All becoming is in time, which is mind. Awakening is outside of time: You awaken from time to That which is timeless."

The first book by Jed McKenna was a treasure of nondual wisdom woven into a series of vignettes centering on a, possibly fictional, enlightened guru operating out of an old farmhouse in Iowa. *Spiritual Enlightenment: The Damnedest Thing* opens on ten pages of rave reviews, which includes the praises of many established authorities in the field of spirituality. McKenna's style of teaching is definitely tough love and many may not enjoy his caustic, confrontational approach to spirituality.

I had read more than a few books on nonduality when I first read *Spiritual Enlightenment* in the summer of 2003. As much as I was drawn to this kind of thinking, it never really clicked for me until about two weeks after I finished his book. At that time, everything opened up and all the books I had read on Zen and Taoism suddenly made perfect sense. I reread *Spiritual Enlightenment* several more times during the next year, along with many other books on nonduality by other authors, such as Eckhart Tolle.

Two major works by Eckhart Tolle have penetrated deeply into the popular market by appealing to the practical needs of seekers. *A New Earth: Awakening to Your Life's Purpose* is a beautiful book that gives the reader guidelines for changing the world, one person at a time. Tolle's choice of title for his book resonates strongly with the shift of consciousness that we will be talking about in the last chapter of this book.

Eckankar was, for me, a spiritual system that employed a variety of nondual teachings, including what it called *contemplation*, which was very similar to one of the mainstays of Zen, sitting mediation or *zazen*. During the first few of my many years with Eckankar, I had two satori experiences that will never be forgotten.

Between my departure from Eckankar in the eighties and the awakening in 2003, I bought only one book by Alan Watts, another copy of *The Wisdom of Insecurity*. Since the awakening, however, I have developed an entirely different perspective that allows me to appreciate Watts at a much deeper level. I learned much from Watts, for he took the ideas of the Far East and spoke them in a way that invaded the structure of my small town, Midwestern, American mind. I just finished reading his autobiography, *In My Own Way,* and though he died young at 58, he lived a full life and left much of value behind.

Challenging Nonduality

Many find nonduality a difficult concept to accept, and as a concept, it does present serious challenges. If you approach the concept of nonduality as a solution to your conceptual problems, you miss the mark, and if it leads anywhere at all, this kind of thinking will likely result in nihilism or solipsism. Nihilism is a philosophy that devalues existence completely, leaving no basis, no reason, and no purpose to anything at all. Solipsism, on the other hand, is the perspective that everything that exists, exists only within "my" mind, leaving no room for the existence of anything outside the mind. To some, nonduality can only appear as one or the other of these choices, but this kind of thing can happen when you try too hard to put non-conceptual truth into concepts.

If, on the other hand, you feel drawn to the idea of nonduality, thinking of it as a concept will not help you much. Understand that the mind defines the reality in which we live, and the mind defines everything in terms of concepts; that is how it is structured. Primary to the creation of a conceptual structure is the concept of a self, and once you have a self, there must be other, and that is duality. As soon as there is a you thought, duality happens. Therefore, it should be clear that "you" are part of duality and cannot escape it or become enlightened. This is why, as Watts said, "you have to go out of your mind." Not exactly crazy, but you have to recognize the ego as just an image, and trust life enough to move away from the idea that the ego must or even can control the unfolding of the story.

What you really are is not this tiny contraction of mental energy called ego, but a function of the universe. Without any input from the ego, your heart beats, your eyes see, the Earth rotates and revolves around the sun, the universe expands, and life goes on. What you really are is an expression of that, and on a grander scale, you are that. All "you" can do is to recognize the realization when the time comes and get out of the way.

"A myth is an image in terms of which
we try to make sense of the World."

Alan Watts

Chapter Four

Logos vs. Mythos

Both of these terms, "logos" and "mythos." are of Greek origin and their polarity can easily be seen in the enduring conflict between science and religion. Logos translates as statement, principle, law, reason, or proportion, but the interpretations vary from field to field. The hard scientist may see logos as the heart of logic and reason, while to the philosopher logos might be the force that drives us to understand the world around us. These views seem quite compatible, but if the scientist or the philosopher is a Christian then logos is also the Word of God, which was made flesh in the form of Jesus Christ. While religion has so declared its own connection to logos, it is more accurately linked to mythos.

Mythos refers to folklore, legend, lore, myth, or mythology, which is generally expressed as stories that describe symbolically or metaphorically the nature of idealized relationships between the individual and the aesthetic, practical, moral, or spiritual values endorsed by the culture. Mythos is the expression of good over evil, however these terms are defined by the presiding culture. Therefore, because it has value in a cultural context, the truth of mythos remains unquestioned and immune to the criticisms of logos.

Myth as Science

Historically, problems arose when mythos made claims about the physical world that could not be supported by reason and logic; the heresy trial of Galileo (1564–1642) jumps to mind, as does the long-standing disagreement between creationism and evolution.

At the time in history when the Catholic Church was near the peak of its power, it was believed that a flat Earth was at the center of God's creation and that the sun, moon and stars revolved around it. This common view of the world was the view held by the Church, and the Church declared it to be the view of God. Galileo, building on the ideas of Copernicus (1473–1543), observed through his telescope that contrary to popular belief, the round Earth was not at the center of creation but revolved around the sun along with the other planets. Galileo announced his discovery and was sent before the Inquisition, charged with heresy and sentenced to an extended house arrest during which he was allowed to continue writing. He could just as easily have been sentenced to death for this crime; defying the authority of the Church during that period could reduce one's lifespan significantly.

The Galileo incident took place in the early 1600's when the power of the Church was near absolute; even kings bowed before his holiness the Pope. By 1859, when Charles Darwin (1809–1882) published *On the Origin of Species by Means of Natural Selection*, the power of the Church was greatly diminished. Nonetheless, Darwin was scorned by the Church and his writings were considered heresy, but such charges were no longer the jurisdiction of the law and he was not imprisoned for his ideas. Though it now stands as the foundation of modern biology, Darwin's work was banned by the Catholic Church until 1950 when its position opened somewhat; in 1996 the Pope issued conditional approval to the theory of evolution. It appears that for the time being the battle between logos and mythos is an unsteady truce. While some issues, such as human cloning and stem cell research, are sensitive subjects, I have heard of no major conflicts between religion and modern physics, but who can say what tomorrow may bring?

Separate but Equal

In our physiology logos relates to the left hemisphere of the brain, which processes information linearly, while mythos, like the right hemisphere, processes images globally. Working together like the left and right hemispheres of the brain, logos takes on the role of accumulating knowledge and organizing systems in the world of the "other," while mythos is the drive that propels consciousness to comprehend the mysteries of existence.

Joseph Campbell, who wrote the book on *The Power of Myth*, saw myth as vital to the existence of humanity. As long as religion remains in the realm of mythology its power contributes to the welfare of humanity by pointing to truth; it is when religion aspires to be considered truth, in a factual or historical sense that problems arise. In the words of Campbell, "Whenever the poetry of myth is interpreted as biography, history, or science, it is killed. The living images become only remote facts of a distant time or place. Furthermore, it is never difficult to demonstrate that as science and history, mythology is absurd." In his work and writing, Campbell has brought to light mythical motifs that arise spontaneously in human culture, many of which are incorporated into Judeo-Christian-Muslim mythology. The Creation, the Garden of Eden, the Chosen People, the flight from slavery, the Great Flood, even the figures of Jesus and Muhammad can be recognized by other names in the mythologies of earlier cultures, as well as cultures that were geographically isolated on other continents, such as the indigenous cultures of the Americas, Australia, and the Pacific islands. Campbell felt that these patterns were ingrained into the human psyche much like the psychological archetypes of Carl Jung, and that under certain circumstances these cultural archetypes would emerge in the form of myths and legends. As has always been the case, myths are expressed as literature and theater, but today we must add the modern venues of television and cinema.

Myth in the Media

The most enduring, most frequently recurring, most inspirational myth must surely be that of the hero's journey. Other than Jesus, of course, one of the first heroes that I remember was Superman; "faster than a speeding bullet, more powerful than a locomotive, able to leap tall buildings in a single bound. Look – up in the sky; it's a bird, it's a plane…" More recently, Thomas Anderson became Neo in the *Matrix* film trilogy where he was born of a machine (not a virgin, but interesting), he studied with masters, learned to perform miracles, and was sacrificed so that mankind might be saved. Same story, new characters, the hero myth lives on.

Hero myths like all myths are metaphors that represent the tendency of a culture to move toward a moral ideal. The moral ideal can vary widely and need not be supported by the broad consensus of mainstream thinking; I am sure that at least some of those who followed Jim Jones (1931–1978) to Guyana considered him a hero. Throughout time, the myths return repeatedly with different names and details fashioned to fit the context of the times. In the context that it is conceived, in the context that it is applied, and in the context that it is interpreted, the myth, the story itself, is culture bound and the moral ideal may be as well, but the mythical motif remains.

Zeitgeist is a German word that roughly translates into English as *Spirit of the Times*. It is also the title of a film by Peter Joseph. Part One of the movie, subtitled *The Greatest Story Ever Told*, which is available on the Internet, begins with an astrological/astronomical explanation of the motif we know as the Son of God myth, which is common to Christianity as well as many other mythologies. He also offers a long list of corollaries for this myth where the central religious figure was: born of a virgin on December 25th, became a teacher, had twelve close followers, was sacrificed in the spring, and resurrected three days later.

The date of the birth is the Winter solstice, the shortest day of the year in the Northern hemisphere. In ancient cultures the sun was recognized as the giver of life and the decreasing length of the day symbolically represented the death of the sun. In the film, the narrator tells of one astronomical interpretation, "The star in the east is Sirius, the brightest star in the night sky, which, on December 24th, aligns with the three brightest stars in Orion's Belt. These three bright stars are called today what they were called in ancient times: The Three Kings. The Three Kings and the brightest star, Sirius, all point to the place of the sunrise on December 25th. This is why the Three Kings 'follow' the star in the east, in order to locate the sunrise – the birth of the sun." The twelve followers of the given hero, in this interpretation, represent the signs of the zodiac.

Following the Winter solstice, the days increase in duration until at the Spring equinox the days become longer than the nights as the light of God conquers darkness, bringing the new growing season and salvation. The spring holiday is celebrated variously in many belief systems as: Alban Eilir, Easter, Eostar, Eostre, Feast of Annunciation of the Blessed Virgin Mary, Festival of Trees, Lady Day, NawRuz, No Ruz, Ostara, Ostra, Passover, Rites of Spring, and the Vernal Equinox.

Is Mythos Obsolete?

In the view of Joseph Campbell and many others, for humans and human culture to be complete they must be influenced by both logos and mythos. Others feel that we have moved into an era that is governed almost entirely by logos; an idea which is strongly supported by the dominance of left brain oriented critical thinking in modern culture.

According to Karen Armstrong in her bestseller, *The Battle for God*, "In the premodern world, both *mythos* and *logos* were regarded as indispensable. Each would be impoverished without the other. Yet the two were essentially distinct, and it was held to be dangerous to confuse mythical and rational discourse. They had separate jobs to do. Myth was not reasonable; its narratives were not supposed to be demonstrated empirically. It provided the context of meaning that made our practical activities worthwhile. You were not supposed to make *mythos* the basis of a pragmatic policy. If you did so, the results could be disastrous, because what worked well in the inner world of the psyche was not readily applicable to the affairs of the external world." She goes on to describe how things have altered since we have come into the current era, "Our religious experience in the modern world has changed, and because an increasing number of people regard scientific rationalism alone as true, they have often tried to turn the *mythos* of their faith into *logos*." In her book, Armstrong talks about the rise of fundamentalism in the twentieth century as an attempt to save mythos by converting it to logos. As pointed out by Campbell, however, to think of a myth in terms of science or history is absurd.

A New Myth

Another view was offered back in the 1960's by Alan Watts who believed that people living in this modern era are likely to be somewhat confused as they are subject to two powerful myths that do not work well together, and neither of which is adequate in fulfilling our needs. In his recorded lecture series, *Out of Your Mind*, Watts described the motifs of these myths as the "ceramic" model, and the "fully automatic" model. "The ceramic model of the universe is based on the book of *Genesis* from which Judaism, Christianity, and Islam devise their basic picture of the world; and the image of the world in the book of *Genesis* is that the world is an artifact. It is made, as a potter takes clay and forms pots out of it, or as a carpenter takes wood and makes tables and chairs out of it." Watts talks about the culture in which the myth developed as he continues, "The ceramic model of the universe originated in cultures where the form of government was monarchical and where, therefore, the maker of the universe was conceived…as the king of the universe." God, the King of kings, was also seen as the maker and enforcer of the law. As lowly peasants, we cannot approach the almighty king, and this view, that we are *unworthy*, works to separate us from God. As Western culture developed, however, new ways of thinking called into question the ideology that had been built around the ceramic myth. As our knowledge and understanding grew, another view of the world emerged.

The fully automatic model is the way of science, and science has observed the universe as processes taking place in regular predictable patterns. The real purpose of science, according to Watts, is to make predictions about the universe, and scientists came to recognize that the idea that *God created and controls the universe* did not contribute to the accuracy of their predictions. While the consistencies that scientists observed in nature did indeed support the idea of laws, the law-maker's services were no longer required and the laws of God were, in most areas of life, replaced by the laws of nature as described by science. Regardless of how much we want to believe in the ideology of the ceramic model because it assuages our fear of death with the idea of life eternal, it is the fully automatic model that more accurately describes the way we experience and observe life. As much as we desire to define reality in terms of the myths handed to us by those whom we love and trust, what we say we believe will very likely be in conflict with what we think we know. What most of us are willing to honestly believe has moved out of the Middle Ages and for many the fully automatic myth has presented a persuasive alternative to the religious traditions of the past.

While the ceramic model places humankind as subservient peasants to the almighty king of the universe, the fully automatic model relegates us to being mere cogs in the blind machinery of existence. Watts believed that neither of these myths effectively describes reality, as both support the position that we are somehow separate things living in a universe of separate things, which, in his view, is definitely not the case. Watts believed in the nonduality of existence, which we discussed in the previous chapter.

To correct this misunderstanding Watts proposed an alternative myth derived from the Hindu teachings that he called the "dramatic" model of the universe. When we employ the dramatic model, we discover that reality is not the battle for survival and security that it often appears to be, but an enactment, a play in which the Absolute plays all the parts. One could think of existence as a game that the universe, God, Brahman, or the Absolute by any other name, plays with itself. From this perspective we see that reality, as we know it, is much like a game of hide and seek in which the formless Absolute, which is nondual, takes on form and becomes hidden in its own manifestation. While the manifestation itself is premised on duality and the perception of separateness and polarities, what we must ultimately realize is that it is the very idea of separateness that creates the illusions of conflict and suffering.

Science as Myth

Watts presents an interesting option to the traditional myths of Western culture, and his dramatic myth might be an acceptable alternative if only it had evolved in typical mythological fashion.

However, we tend not to choose our myths but inherit them through tradition, and unfortunately, in Western culture, the dramatic myth lacks both history and mystery (though Hindus might find it familiar). Nevertheless, perhaps another possibility exists within the words of Watts; while religion makes bold claims with regards to issues of logos as the *Word* of God, science is reticent to admit that it is, as Watts tells us, a myth in its own right. I suggest that the fully automatic myth, which Watts characterizes as the way of science, should not be written off without consideration. The question is, can we really fit a path of logos into a believable new mythology?

According to Watts, it has already been done in the fully automatic model. We treat science like a myth; most of us accept scientific thinking as true without understanding exactly how it works, and there are mysteries that even the scientists do not comprehend. In the form of the sciences logos has a history that goes back at least as far as ancient Greece, it has heroes and villains, it presents a coherent description of reality as we experience it, it has elements of mystery and suspense, and there is a sense of almost divine justice in the idea of cause and effect. The latest developments in many branches of science, such as medicine, must surely stand as miracles in some sense; and subatomic physics has come to understand that the entire universe is connected as if it were one infinite eternal organism. Science is a myth that works because it is curious rather than dogmatic, it is a myth that grows to encompasses life rather than restricting it with ideas like sin. The "Word of God," like the Absolute, is not carved in stone, but is written in the unfolding of consciousness, it is living and growing, it is the present moment changing unceasingly, it is pure awareness without content, it is *what is*, right here, right now.

And what of our protagonist; where does Sophia Perennis stand on logos versus mythos? First we must understand that logos and mythos are a polarity, as are the subjects of all the chapters in *Part II, Polarities*, and as humans we have adapted to this world where reality exists only as relationships between opposing concepts. Sophia recognizes that any polarity presents contrasts, and that the mind is drawn to contrasts and other shiny things. In such a reality as this, it is only natural that all human minds will have certain preferences and opinions based on conditioned beliefs about the world. Though the proposed idea of logos *as* mythos is a path the seeker could take, what Sophia points to is the end of seeking. As we will see in the next few chapters, Sophia is not captivated by any polarity, but stands in the objective middle ground that is unaffected by the poles.

*"Every religion is true one way or another.
It is true when understood metaphorically.
But when it gets stuck in its own metaphors,
interpreting them as facts, then you are in trouble."*

Joseph Campbell

Chapter Five

Exoteric vs. Esoteric

The terms "exoteric" and "esoteric" are Greek in origin and refer to the adjective form of outer (exo) and inner (eso). One could say that exoteric teachings emphasize the outward physical actions of life through which we relate to other, while esoteric paths focus on the inner subjective parts, like thinking and feeling wherein we relate to the higher aspects within ourselves. In modern usage, both terms generally refer to established belief systems that we call religions.

Exoteric religions are those geared to the masses and which promise a reward to the faithful in some afterlife. Most people who claim to be Jewish, Christian or Muslim follow an exoteric path. Exoteric systems tend to be highly structured, and extend that structure into the lives of their members by prescribing moral and ethical standards of behavior. Scripture is considered the inerrant Word of God, and rewards and punishments for certain behaviors are prescribed therein. Exoteric systems are commonly referred to as *organized religion*, as they are hierarchical in structure, and the authority for interpreting scripture and setting policy is generally placed with a highly positioned individual or council within the organization, then distributed to clergy who administer policy, officiate at worship services, and tend to the spiritual needs of their congregations. Using the power of their membership, the exoteric religions impose behavioral standards on culture at large and, in doing so, gain the support of the political structure. In the exoteric perspective, how one lives in this life determines how one will spend forever; therefore, their lives are firmly rooted in memories of the past and aimed at an idealized future.

Traditionally esoteric teachings were hidden, and their practice was limited to small groups. Today, they still do not usually appeal to the masses of casual seekers, but are very attractive to the growing number of people who want truth above all else. All of these paths generally believe, in some sense, that there is divinity at the core of the individual, and that by reaching this core we can realize the divinity of the Absolute. In practice, these teachings are as diverse as are those of the exoteric paths, but the emphasis is on merging with divinity rather than salvation of the individual soul.

The Traditionalist View

In the first half of the twentieth century, René Guénon was the leading figure in the rediscovery of Sophia Perennis, followed closely by religious scholar Frithjof Schuon. These two and their followers became known as the Traditionalist School of philosophy, and they point out that Western religions are practiced as both exoteric and esoteric systems. This structure gives rise to two disparate expressions of spirituality.

In Schuon's book, *The Transcendent Unity of Religions*, we read of his view on the differences between exoteric and esoteric religion. "Exotericism may be said to be founded on the 'creature-Creator' dualism to which it attributes an absolute reality," and he refers to the exoteric perspective as, "an irreducible dualism and the exclusive pursuit of individual salvation – this dualism implying that God is considered solely under the aspect of His relationship with the created and not in His total and infinite Reality, in His Impersonality, which annihilates all apparent reality other than Him." It appears that the exoteric religions, by focusing on this requirement for a personal God who is involved in and judges human affairs, have devalued, if not completely dismissed, any need for an awareness of the Absolute that exceeds their personal desire for salvation in the afterlife. The exoteric teachings dwell on the separation of humanity from God and pursue the appropriate means of achieving individual salvation in the afterlife.

Of the esoterics Schuon writes, "The perspective of the esoteric doctrines shows up with particular clarity in their way of regarding what is commonly called 'evil'; it has often been said that they deny evil purely and simply, but such an interpretation is too rudimentary and expresses the perspective of the doctrines in question in a very imperfect manner." Schuon goes on to explain that in the esoteric view, evil is simply a way of defining a function of the whole on the basis of individual human interest. In the esoteric view, evil truly exists solely in the mind and, as a function of the ultimate reality, is not judged.

Schuon is difficult to quote on esotericism because when he writes on subjects of such great depth his sentences tend to be quite complex and longer than most people's paragraphs. In the *Introduction to the Revised Edition* of Schuon's book, fellow religious scholar Huston Smith adds this simple explanation, "The esoteric minority consists of men and women who realize that they have their roots in the Absolute. Either they experience the identification directly or, failing this, they stand within earshot of its claim; something within them senses that the claim is true even if they cannot validate it completely. The exoteric majority is composed of the remainder of mankind for whom this way of talking about religion is sterile if not unintelligible."

Achieving the sense of unity with God as sought by the esoteric is not often realized, but especially by those on the exoteric paths; alas, union with God is nondual and that is not what is being sought or taught in the exoteric systems. Realizing the eternal peace of being one with God is incomprehensible to the mind; no doubt for what were deemed good and practical reasons, the idea of unity was replaced by the promise of remaining a perfected individual and being in the company of God forever.

The Creation of Evil

In *Thou Art That* Joseph Campbell looks at this issue a little differently as he refers to the ethical perspective and the mystical perspective, "There are two orders of religious perspective. One is ethical, pitting good against evil. In the biblically grounded Christian West, the accent is on ethics, on good against evil. We are thus bound by our religion itself to the field of duality. The mystical perspective, however, views good and evil as aspects of one process.

"We have, then, these two totally different religious perspectives. The idea of good and evil absolutes in the world after the fall is biblical and as a result, you do not rest on corrupted nature. Instead, you correct nature and align yourself with the good against evil. Eastern cults, on the other hand, put you in touch with nature, where what the Westerners call good and evil interlock. But by what right, this Eastern tradition asks, do we call these things evil when they are of the process of nature?" This is exactly the esoteric perspective, whereas the view left to Western culture by its religions is that nature, both externally and our own inner nature as human beings, is a force to be overcome and controlled for the greater good.

As a system of ethics, the focus of exoteric religions is to control behavior for the greater good, which includes repressing those pesky natural instincts and urges that the doctrine considers sinful or negative. The teachings of Jesus did not stress this perspective, neither in the canonical gospels nor in the Gnostic gospels discovered in the mid twentieth century. The idea of sinfulness emerges primarily in writings attributed to Paul and dominates the Christian canon with ideas of sin and repentance. Later St. Augustine introduced the concept of original sin, which further defined the nature of humanity as sinful and bound for eternal damnation in hell, but for the grace of God and belief in Jesus Christ as the son of God and savior of humankind.

Once we accept this damning view of humanity as true, the idea of salvation becomes very attractive, and the power of exoteric religion to control the behavior and even the thoughts of the individual is nearly complete. Even for those who may not embrace all elements of the doctrine, general compliance is relatively easy, and absolution is readily available when you mess up. This is the basis for the famous wager proposed by Blaise Pascal (1623–1662), which states that it is logical to believe in the Christian God, for if God exists and the teachings of Christianity are true, the cost of not believing in God (hell) is greater than the cost of believing in God if He does not exist.

However, as our understanding of reality expands through scientific rationalism and the unfolding of current events, this proposition becomes increasingly harder to justify.

Hero Worship

An attractive aspect of exoteric religion is the fantastic stories that lay out the myths that many take to be the history of the belief system. As part of their journey, the heroes of these tales experience, and inspire in others, divine revelations and miracles that confirm and support the teaching of the path. Only when one steps off the path, however, can these myths, and the effect they have on the followers, be examined objectively, as was done by Śankara Śaranam in his book, *God Without Religion: Questioning Centuries of Accepted Truth.* "Against the gray backdrop of today's apparent chaos and cynicism, there is special allure in identifying with the heroic men and women of religious texts. Their lives may appear more black and white, and their days less burdened with complex decision-making. Idealizing these epic figures, many people see them as better and wiser than us, and their societies as more cohesive. Adoption of their revelatory perspective follows naturally. But while swept up in romantic illusions of the past, and having surrendered their own intellectual faculties, these individuals often fail to consider that their scriptural heroes and heroines, routinely shaped by social and religious forces often alien to our own, are mythic inventions of the human imagination."

Worshiping God

When I was just a small child, I was told that the Christian God was, omniscient, omnipotent, and omnipresent. All knowing, all power-ful, and everywhere at once; to me that meant that everything that exists, pretty much exists as a part or a function of God. From this idea I concluded that prayer was, in a sense, talking to yourself, and I could accept that explanation as I knew people did that frequently. The idea of worship, however, didn't really fit at all. If, indeed, God was all that the Church claimed, how could anything exist outside of God? Who, or what, I wondered, was the object of this worship?

Elsewhere in his book, Śaranam explains the function of worship very nicely. "Religious authorities also advise congregants seeking knowledge of God to faithfully attend worship services. In these settings, their awareness is drawn outward toward the congregation, ceremonial events, and the art and architecture of the house of worship. But when the self's avenue to intuitive knowledge is directed outward, dividing into currents that feed the five senses, the individual ends up worshipping the narrow, individuated self as defined by sensory information. By contrast, when the avenue to knowledge is directed inward the person is able to worship indivisible being. The first instance leads to all manner of idolatry, or worship of atom-based realities circumscribed by space and time, while the second leads to what the ancients called isolation, union with the infinite substance of self as one's own self beyond all causal ideas of division. Worship services, by virtue of their emphasis on cognitive faculties, fall short of expectations because in directing attention to finite sensory objects one cannot acquire knowledge of an infinite God as one's self.

"The most a person can do during 'outer worship' is engage in a disguised form of self-worship. People often worship themselves by worshipping individuals with whom they identify. Revering Muhammad, for example, amounts to revering oneself identified with a Muhammad that reflects the self's parameters. Identifying with a book and calling it holy is another means of canonizing oneself and one's opinions."

God of the Gaps

One of the primary functions of religion has always been to provide a way to comprehend the mysteries of life, which religion attempts to do by ascribing these mysteries to a deity and giving it a name. At various times in our history, humans believed in gods of the harvest, gods of rain, sun gods and gods for all the parts of life that we did not understand and could not control, but in Western religion there is only one God to fill all these gaps. In modern times, we find that the "God of the gaps" has fewer and fewer arenas that we cannot account for more efficiently by rational thinking, and the accumulation of scientific knowledge continues to narrow what gaps remain.

Exoteric vs. Esoteric

Exoteric religions rest on the principle of separation, which is reinforced by the culture at large, and the culture, in turn, benefits from the admonitions of the Church. With the emphasis on becoming better rather than being what they are, followers of exoteric paths tend to be invested in outcomes that affect the relationship between self and other, and seem to be motivated primarily by what they believe is outside the self. Those who follow the esoteric paths participate in duality simply because it is, as they are, as everything is – a manifestation of the Divine; there is no other and no self, no doer only doing, only *All That Is*.

Chapter Six

Good vs. Evil

These are familiar words that most everyone will claim to understand to some extent. Good, when defined as an adjective usually indicates the desirable position of a thing or action on a scale of value, usefulness or some quality at the other end of which is "bad." (good, better, best/bad, worse, worst) When defined as a noun it is seen as a thing or event possessing qualities described by the adjective "good." (the good, the bad and the ugly) Most would agree that the concept of evil is bad, but whether used as an adjective or a noun, evil implies a moral or ethical quality, the opposite of which might be "virtuous," "righteous," or "holy." We may casually refer to natural disasters, bad drivers, crab grass and other things we don't like as evil, but it is usually a conscious exaggeration; most often what we call evil is brought about by malicious intent.

Through careless common usage, extending from the vernacular to academia, these words have become entwined in our culture and in our minds as being in direct opposition when, in fact, their opposition is somewhat skewed. The word "good" refers to a condition of value and the word "evil" is defined as a measure or lack of virtue. An argument could be made that value and virtue overlap to some degree in their meanings; but they are not the same. Value is first and foremost a functional measure while virtue is a moral category. An abortion or euthanasia may improve the situation of all involved, thereby being a good thing, but it is unlikely that any fundamentalist would call these virtuous acts. Likewise, a sacrifice made in vain may be considered a virtue to the extent that it could even result in a negative effect. Yet we may still consider the act itself to be virtuous, although no measure of good can be claimed other than possibly intent; and we all know what the road to hell is paved with. It is my opinion that when we place good and evil on the same scale we jeopardize our understanding of both terms. However, since history has considered them a polarity we shall as well, but perhaps a little less seriously than most.

The Problem of Good & Evil

For centuries humans have debated, especially in the arena of religious philosophy, what is known as *the problem of good and evil*. In this context, the all powerful, all knowing God of Western religion, specifically the Christian God, is assumed to be the ultimate good. The question that automatically arises from this assumption is, "If God is ultimately good and all powerful, how can there exist that which we call evil?" In an Internet article entitled *The Problem of Good and Evil: How can a Good God Allow Evil?* found at Leadership University's Christian based website, author Rick Rood addresses the standard logical argument as follows:

"The logical challenge is usually posed in the form of a statement such as this:

1. "A good God would destroy evil.

2. "An all powerful God could destroy evil.

3. "Evil is not destroyed.

4. "Therefore, there cannot possibly be such a good and powerful God.

"It is logically impossible to believe that both evil, and a good and powerful God exist in the same reality, for such a God certainly could and would destroy evil.

"On the other hand, the evidential challenge contends that while it may be rationally possible to believe such a God exists, it is highly improbable or unlikely that He does. We have evidence of so much evil that is seemingly pointless and of such horrendous intensity. For what valid reason would a good and powerful God allow the amount and kinds of evil which we see around us?

"These issues are of an extremely important nature – not only as we seek to defend our belief in God, but also as we live out our Christian lives."

After quoting David Hume (1711–1776) and three passages from *The Bible*, Rood concludes with the following defenses against the above logical argument to the question "How can a Good God Allow Evil?": 1.) "He cannot do anything that is 'out of character' for a righteous God," and 2.) "Creatures who are free to follow His will, must also be free to reject it. And when people act in ways outside the will of God, great evil and suffering is the ultimate result."

While this type of response is typical, neither defense to this logical argument is logical. Firstly, he assumes that "good God" and "righteous God" are synonymous, and considering the current state of affairs in the world, this may not be a warranted assumption. Muslim extremists believe it is righteous to kill infidels, but we infidels here in the United States think that if the Muslim extremists are not evil then they must surely be crazy. Good and evil have nothing to do with Ein Sof, Jehovah, Allah, or the Absolute by any other name, but are judgments in the minds of individuals, religions, cultures, and humanity as a species. We extend and validate our individuality by identifying with those who share our definitions of good and evil, and by doing so in the name of religion we hope to validate our individuality into eternity.

To accept his second defense we must stipulate to the existence of free will, which not only confounds the notions of an "all knowing" and "all powerful" God, but the existence of free will is itself a hotly contested philosophical assertion. (see the next chapter on free will) The short and most obvious logical conclusion is that the question, "How can a Good God Allow Evil?" is actually a contradiction based on at least one faulty premise. To resolve this longstanding problem we must first understand that God, defined as the Absolute, is all-inclusive and cannot be limited or divided by the opinions of mere mortals regarding what is good and what is evil.

Defining Evil

In *Remedial Christianity* Paul Alan Laughlin lays out four different approaches to the idea of evil as found in the Christian scriptures. Earthquakes and tsunamis are certainly bad for the victims, but in the geological perspective they are simply part of the process that is the development of the planet. Natural events and human actions are judged by humans as either good or bad based on how we are affected by them. These judgments are in no way absolute, even though our convictions may be quite powerful; it is in this sense that evil is relative and seen as "a Value Judgment."

Plotinus was the philosopher who founded the Neo-Platonist school that was based on many of the teachings of Plato (428–347 BCE). The ideas of Plotinus were very popular during the time when Christianity was developing as an ideology and it left a heavy mark on the tone of Christian doctrine. Plato did not accept the relativistic position on evil but declared that there are perfect positive ideals, which he called forms, and that what we perceive as negatives are a lack of goodness or a deviation from the perfect positive form. Where the case of evil as a value judgment sees evil as something that is bad for someone; evil when viewed as "a Deprivation of/Deviation from the Good" is independent of personal judgment as the Good is seen, not as a mere opinion, but as a philosophical ideal.

All Western religions are concerned with the issue of evil, but the Jewish tradition best preserves the idea of monotheism by considering evil as emanating from the same God who gives us good. Good and evil are viewed as God's blessings and God's punishments. In the Hebrew tradition, Satan is portrayed, not as the embodiment of evil so much as an agent of God. Laughlin points out how sometimes what we think of as evil is referenced in our everyday language as "acts of God," or "God's will." The evil of the Old Testament was attributed, not to a force of evil, but to God. In this third sense God is the source of all and evil is "an Attribute/Aspect of the Good."

Early Christians decided that God should not be seen as responsible for evil and declared God the ultimate ideal good in the Neo-Platonist sense. Evil as "a deviation from the good", however, was not substantial enough to justify the "Fall of Man;" so it was necessary that evil become a negative force separate from God, the ideal good. Laughlin clearly summarizes this view of evil in saying, "From the New Testament writers on, Christians have identified that negative force as Satan, and have treated Satan (in a very un-Jewish way) as the Devil, a definite power and agent of evil who opposes God's will, resists God's power, and threatens God's people. In so doing, Christians have maintained a fourth view of evil (besides that of relativism, Platonism, and Judaism). They have taught that evil is a separate, countervailing power or force over against the good; and they generally have ignored the challenge that this view presents for their claim that there is only one God." Based on the doctrine as it is taught and practiced, a God that is ultimately good by Christian standards could never be more than half a God in this world of duality.

A Catholic View

The Roman Catholic position is often very different from the protestant views which are more familiar to me, so I checked with the Catholic Online Encyclopedia (COE) to see if it had something more to add on this topic. While there was no specific entry for "the problem of good and evil," I found an extensive analysis of both "good" and "evil" that exceeded my expectations by including quotes from, not just Hume and *The Bible*, but many other philosophical sources as well. As we have discussed, Western theology was highly influenced by Plato and Plotinus whose ideas were well represented in the article; also quoted were many philosophers from the Middle Ages when virtually everyone agreed with the Church because disagreeing with the Church could be fatal. A few important philosophers from more recent times, including Leibniz (1646–1716), Nietzsche (1844–1900), and Schopenhauer are sourced as well. It came as no surprise, however, that the majority of quotes came from the words of saints and especially from scripture, as for the believer, scripture is the Word if God. The entries are well referenced within the original text by liberal use of parentheses and brackets, but excerpts quoted here will not include those references.

All these references to other viewpoints, including some references to Eastern nondual teachings, was admirably open minded, but what I was really looking for was a simple, 100% truly Catholic perspective. Perhaps it is my own bias at work, but I was unable to find a concise Catholic definition of evil that was clearly delineated from the other views offered. I was able to extract these few relevant comments regarding the Catholic view of evil:

"Christian philosophy has, like the Hebrew, uniformly attributed moral and physical evil to the action of created free will. Man has himself brought about the evil from which he suffers by transgressing the law of God, on obedience to which his happiness depended. Evil is in created things under the aspect of mutability, and possibility of defect, not as existing *per se*: and the errors of mankind, mistaking the true conditions of its own well-being, have been the cause of moral and physical evil. The evil from which man suffers is, however, the condition of good, for the sake of which it is permitted. Thus, 'God judged it better to bring good out of evil than to suffer no evil to exist'. Evil contributes to the perfection of the universe, as shadows to the perfection of a picture, or harmony to that of music. Again, the excellence of God's works in nature is insisted on as evidence of the Divine wisdom, power, and goodness, by which no evil can be directly caused. Thus Boethius asks Who can be the author of good, if God is the author of evil? As darkness is nothing but the absence of light, and is not produced by creation, so evil is merely the defect of goodness. St. Basil points out the educative purposes served by evil; and St. Augustine, holding evil to be permitted for the punishment of the wicked and the trial of the good, shows that it has, under this aspect, the nature of good, and is pleasing to God, not because of what it is, but because of where it is; i.e. as the penal and just consequence of sin. Lactantius uses similar arguments to oppose the dilemma, as to the omnipotence and goodness of God, which he puts into the mouth of

Epicurus. St. Anselm connects evil with the partial manifestation of good by creation; its fullness being in God alone.

"The features which stand out in the earlier Christian explanation of evil, as compared with non-Christian dualistic theories are thus:

- "the definite attribution to God of absolute omnipotence and goodness, notwithstanding His permission of the existence of evil;

- "the assignment of a moral and retributive cause for suffering in the sin of mankind; and

- "the unhesitating assertion of the beneficence of God's purpose in permitting evil, together with the full admission that He could, had He so chosen, have prevented it."

In the view presented here, evil is simply the shadow of goodness, or the absence of goodness, which cannot be considered evil in its own right, but only in relation to human activity. The deification of an ideal Good is, in theory, a philosophy with which most people could live, especially if it was integral to their culture. As practiced in duality, however, ideologies that claim a monopoly on good, define all that is not included in their belief system as varying degrees of evil. It was precisely this type of thinking that led to all the wars and other carnage committed in the name of religion. It is why the behavior of Muslims seems so strange to most Christians, and why fundamentalist Muslims believe that all infidels must be converted or eliminated.

Indeed, evil is not a natural state but comes about as we separate ourselves from the Oneness that is God, and identify with the conditioned judgments we make about ourselves, others, and the world at large, as well as judgments we make about God. This is a relatively simple idea, but leave it to the mind of man to complicate things. The following excerpt, also from the COE, shows what can happen when truth is overlaid with ideology and dogma:

"In the light of Catholic doctrine, any theory that may be held concerning evil must include certain points bearing on the question (sic) that have been authoritatively defined. These points are

- "the omnipotence, omniscience, and absolute goodness of the Creator;
- "the freedom of the will; and
- "that suffering is the penal consequence of willful disobedience to the law of God.

"A complete account may be gathered from the teaching of St. Thomas Aquinas, by whom the principles of St. Augustine are systematized, and to some extent supplemented. Evil, according to St. Thomas, is a privation, or the absence of some good which belongs properly to the nature of the creature. There is therefore no "summum malum", or positive source of evil, corresponding to the "summum bonum", which is God; evil being not "ens reale" but only "ens rationis" – i.e. it exists not as an objective fact, but as a subjective conception; things are evil not in themselves, but by reason of their relation to other things, or persons. All realities *(entia)* are in themselves good; they produce bad results only incidentally; and consequently the ultimate cause of evil if (sic) fundamentally good, as well as the objects in which evil is found."

Again, St. Augustine, with help from St. Aquinas (1225–1274), was on the scene to help clear things up. Are you clear on how this works? It seems that while God is the source of absolute Good, evil has no source but is merely a concept that arises in human activity. One thing we can certainly see in the Christian view is that free will in humans is tightly linked to the ideas of sin and the nature of evil. Free will is of great importance to both the religions and cultures of Western civilization and free will is the subject of the next chapter.

Fade to Relativism

In our modern world, we witness a collapse of these notions of evil as they fall into each other under the weight of global communications and economic pressures. We have built our world culture based on a medium of exchange, so the additional influence of international financial factors in setting government policy is unavoidable. There have always been either blatant or thinly veiled economic reasons beyond the stated humanitarian and political justifications for wars throughout history. Beginning with the Vietnam conflict in the mid twentieth century, wars have been televised and exposed in the print media and on television for the world to see. Now, the Internet makes information about events and people all over the planet even more accessible. The world is so interconnected that nothing moves without everything moving and the whole idea of good and evil breaks down to the relativistic form, that is to say that today most people realize that how we define good and evil is only a matter of preference.

There are too many differing opinions to define an ideal Good in the Platonistic sense, and attributing evil to Acts of God has given way to blaming, and possibly suing, others, while the God of goodness concept remains to threaten the monotheistic ground on which all of Western civilization is founded. Perhaps is it time to admit that we are not in a *good* place and ask ourselves, "Where do we go from here?"

"Man is a masterpiece of creation if for no other reason than that, all the weight of evidence for determinism notwithstanding, he believes he has free will."

Georg C. Lichtenberg

Chapter Seven

Free Will vs. Determinism

Like many who will be reading this book, I was born in the United States, a country that was founded on the concept of freedom. Freedom in a world of causality is never complete, however, as both nature and societies have rules. We are not free to break the laws of physics and there are consequences for breaking the laws of governments. Therefore, at the outset we see that in a universe where there is physical and social order, freedom cannot be absolute.

The universe is a system, and within the system there are consistent patterns that we have observed and call the laws or rules of nature. Humans, as subsystems of the universe, are also subject to rules, and we search out these rules to help us understand and make predictions about our world. When we think of freedom, we think of acting according to our own will rather than following the path of determinism or law. Freedom, then, in this world of duality, is the result of free will. It will appear obvious to most people that as we move through life we make choices and take actions that we attribute to free will. It is our experience that by making decisions and acting accordingly we guide the course of our existence in a direction of our choosing.

Determinism comes in various flavors, such as causal determinism, which is the idea that an inevitable future emerges as the direct result of events in the past and present. Similarly, logical determinism holds that all propositions about the past, present, or future are either true or false. Biological determinism says that genetics is the factor that controls all that we do, while theological determinism believes that, through either omniscience or decree, God determines human activity. Many other distinct flavors of determinism have been defined, as well as combinations of flavors.

In a broad definition, though, determinism is the path of causation, and as with our sense of free will, our experience tells us this is true. The classic example of cause and effect, in the physical realm, is the action of billiard balls; when a ball is struck by the cue it moves, when the cue ball hits another ball, that ball moves, etc. Determinism allows everything in our world to exist, it is among the first orders of structure that our minds understand, and the dependability of determinism is the foundation of physical life. Determinism says that nothing happens without a reason and, like free will, determinism seems to be a common sense sort of thing.

Here's the Rub

Many deep thinkers, however, believe these two concepts to be mutually exclusive. The predicament being that while determinism is what appears to keep order in the universe and make it predictable, by definition, free will negates determinism. This apparent incompatibility has been a passionately debated issue since the time of the early Greeks and the discussion rages on as both concepts are integral to how we experience life. There is, as we will see, a wealth of evidence from a variety of disciplines indicating that the concept of free will may not be valid at all, and certainly not to the extent that we seem to experience it.

Free Will and Our Bodies

Let us begin our discussion with an important experiment affecting our understanding of free will that was conducted in the 1970's, by Benjamin Libet (1916–2007), a physiologist, then at the University of California, San Francisco. In order to record their "brainwaves," Libet connected the brains of volunteers to an electroencephalograph and told the subjects to respond to various signals by making "voluntary" motions, such as pressing a button or flicking a finger, while he monitored the time on a very accurate clock. The results showed that brain signals from the motor area associated with the movements themselves occurred almost half a second before the signals in other areas of the brain indicating that the subject was conscious of deciding to make the movement. The sequence of observations was action followed by decision, rather than the other way around. The conscious brain claimed responsibility for what the unconscious brain was already doing; the "decision" to act was literally an afterthought. These results have been reproduced again and again by different researchers, along with other experiments confirming that people can be easily deceived when it comes to assuming ownership of their actions.

Libet offers some measure of consolation to those who favor free will by conceding that his results leave room for a limited form of free will that allows for a degree of veto power over what we sense ourselves doing. As a concession to Western ethical standards he points out that most of the Ten Commandments are "shalt nots."

Free Will in Physics

Among the many contributions of Isaac Newton (1642–1727) was a view of life that is fundamentally deterministic. There is much prima fascia evidence for determinism in our world; we see cause and effect working every minute of every day of our lives. In the world of our senses, determinism dominates the way that our experience unfolds, highly structured and in consistent, predictable patterns; so say the laws of nature. While determinism seems to be the way of the world that we experience directly, in the world of subatomic particles the same rules do not always apply.

The Uncertainty Principle theorized by quantum physicist Werner Heisenberg (1901–1976) opened the door to legitimate scientific speculation regarding free will. It was a simple idea with far reaching implications. In a nut shell, it states that one cannot precisely know both the momentum and position of a subatomic particle simultaneously. The most significant conclusion I draw from this statement is that we cannot completely know the ground state from which an event unfolds. This prevents us from predicting any outcome beyond a measure of probability.

The Heisenberg Uncertainty Principal was closely followed by the work of Erwin Schrödinger (1887–1961), who showed us that matter can be described as either particles or waves, using the same equation. The idea that came out of this line of thought is that before it is observed, matter and energy are best described as a wave function that exists only as a probability. The upshot of this idea is that we cannot prove that anything exists prior to observation.

Because consciousness must be a factor when there is observation, many, especially in New Age circles, have taken this as support for the idea that consciousness creates reality, ergo there is free will. Both the Heisenberg Uncertainty Principal and the Schrödinger Equation rest primarily on the idea of randomness, however, which is not something that we normally associate with consciousness. Still, the apparent random effect could be the result of a measure that is knowable but currently unknown. Most likely, the answer, and its usefulness to humanity, lies somewhere between free will and determinism. I suspect that the majority of physicists and others who give thought to these matters believe that they function in a deterministic universe, while acting as if they have free will.

In another view, the Christian Neuroscience Society offers an article on their web site that claims scientific belief in determinism is due to a misunderstanding, "theoretical physicists show a profound misunderstanding of what free will is. The human will is not a random action, dependent upon quantum uncertainty or a toss of a player's dice. It is the free choice of the human will, as it is determined by the intellect. It is a not a human will determined by the material causality of an instinctual nature. Rather, it is free (whence the term 'free' will) from material causality, and it finds its efficient causality in intellectual self-determination.

"Brute animals have a will but it is not materially free, because they lack an immaterial intellect. On the other hand, man is endowed with an intellect, so man has a rational will. A mentally deranged person has a propensity to act indeterminately and randomly. But, the decisions of an irrational person are not the prototypical examples of the decisions of a person who is considered to be making free-willed decisions." One should not be surprised that a Christian viewpoint would, one way or another, validate free will, as it is an essential part of the doctrine. What I read here is that because we are intelligent (have an immaterial intellect), that the rational type of thinking we do creates free will. I think that rather than proving that free will exists, this argument starts with the assumption that free will exists, but that only certain types of thinking can engage it.

Try as we may, however, a complete scientific explanation of free will, has yet to come forth. Humanity has approached this issue from every conceivable angle, because we want so badly to believe that we control our lives; that the meaning of life must lie in some future purpose that we can move toward with volition.

Philosophically Speaking

To explore free will and determinism as a philosophical issue we must look at things a little differently. According to the Routledge Encyclopedia of Philosophy it is best to not consider the will directly but to broach the topic by asking two specific questions about ourselves: 1) Are we free agents? and, 2) Can we be morally responsible for what we do? Those who believe that free will and determinism are compatible will answer yes to both questions. In this view, free will is essentially just a matter of not being constrained or hindered in certain ways when one acts or chooses. Others point out that since determinism is obviously true, everything that happens was determined to happen at the Big Bang, first cause, or whenever this all began, and no one can be considered truly free or morally responsible for anything.

The moral aspect of this argument presents an enormous ethical dilemma because there is a longstanding precedent that if the perpetrator of an illegal act cannot be held morally responsible then there is no crime. Insanity, temporary insanity, and diminished capacity are valid defenses against any criminal charges if the offender is not of sound mind, and in this case, "sound mind" specifically refers to being responsible for one's actions. The arguments against free will and, by association, moral responsibility, seem very strong, but for most of us, the experience of choice gives rise to a prevailing certainty of owning one's deeds that is immune to scientific or philosophical scrutiny.

Humans require structure in order to make sense of the world; while determinism is basic to our structure of the universe, free will also functions as a structuring device as it affords an accounting of events based on individual responsibility. This sense of moral responsibility is central to the occupation of Western culture and is equally essential to the meaning of Western religion. The Western religious view of free will, therefore, is an important part of the culture, but carries with it certain baggage. Integral to the Western religious view of free will is the idea of sin, so as we examine free will in a religious context we must also consider the concept of sin.

The Idea of Sin

In the context of Western religion, the idea of sin implies that there are fixed conditions of right and wrong that were written down long ago and declared to be the Word of God. Sin is an action or thought that is in violation of God's Law, which is recorded as the doctrine of the Church. Moral responsibility is a requirement of modern civilization, for without it there is no accountability, and without accountability, there is no basis for judging and controlling the behavior of others. We have come to believe that because of our sinful human nature, behavior must be controlled for the greater good. In the doctrine of Western religion, without free will there could be no sin, without sin there would be no guilt, without guilt there is no redemption, and without redemption, Western religion would have no power and little purpose.

Paul Alan Laughlin writes in *Remedial Christianity* about how this doctrine was formed; "The trick was to show how sin had emerged, but without attributing its inception to God; or, in other words, to figure out how to blame sin on humanity without implying a design flaw that made the Creator culpable." How fortuitous that St. Augustine was there to interpret the Old Testament story of the Garden of Eden to mean that humanity was born in sin and that it is human nature to be sinful.

Free Will vs. Determinism

In *Breaking the Spell: Religion as a Natural Phenomenon,* contemporary American philosopher, Daniel C. Dennett finds this perspective on humanity troubling. "Religion plays its most important role in supporting morality, many think, by giving people an unbeatable reason to do good: the promise of an infinite reward in heaven, and (depending on tastes) the threat of an infinite punishment in hell if they don't. Without the divine carrot and stick, goes this reasoning, people would loll about aimlessly or indulge their basest desires, break their promises, cheat on their spouses, neglect their duties, and so on." The two major fallacies with this reasoning are that it doesn't seem to be true, and it is a very demeaning view of our nature. Believing in Heaven and Hell doesn't seem to stop anyone from doing "evil," and in support of his position Dennett points out that prison populations show a similar demographic distribution regarding religious affiliation, or lack thereof, as does the general population.

Sin, in the Christian sense, is the result of God granting humankind the ability to choose the will of God over the sinful human will. Free will, in the Christian view, is essentially a choice between our sinful nature and the preservation of our immortal souls. This presents a serious predicament for Western civilization, for while our knowledge system considers free will at best a personal choice and at worst a relentless fantasy, our belief system considers it the fulcrum on which rests the fate of our eternal existence.

Responsibility

Many feel that freedom and responsibility are two sides of the same coin, and indeed they are connected; freedom being defined as "the ability to act without restraint," and responsibility "to consider the effect of your freedom on others." Responsibility is the primary limitation imposed on freedom by civilization and culture. While culture implies the ideal perspective as a compromise between freedom and responsibility, individual perspectives will appear throughout the spectrum from complete irresponsibility, which society considers highly dysfunctional, to a life of selfless servitude determined by the wishes or needs of others.

Another view of responsibility is offered by Stanley Sobottka, Professor Emeritus of Physics at the University of Virginia, who tackles this and many other subjects relevant to our discussion in *A Course in Consciousness*, which is distributed freely as a book on his web site. *A Course in Consciousness*, by Professor Sobottka, is a blessing to those like me who have sought truth through science. It is a challenge to find documents like this one, which look at the whole of reality, and explain why things appear to be separate, and discuss them in an authoritative, rational, way. In *Chapter 15: Free will and responsibility*, Sobottka points out that, "The tendency to assign or to assume total responsibility regardless of the actual degree of freedom in the choice places the chooser in a hopeless double bind. It seems that the only way to escape one's heredity and conditioning is to assert one's free will, yet free will is never possible because of one's heredity and conditioning.

"In some dualistic New Age teachings, in particular in *A Course in Miracles* (ACIM) and in the 'Seth' books of Jane Roberts, the double bind is escaped by simply asserting that <u>all</u> choices are totally free! Thus, the traditional concept of responsibility has been expanded to state that <u>everything</u> at all times that happens to an individual is a result of choices freely made, and that one must accept responsibility for one's entire life. This implies that one's heredity and environment are also a result of choice. The superficial advantage of adopting this point of view is that there is no room left for any ambiguity in accepting responsibility, and there is never any justification whatsoever in blaming anybody or anything else for one's own lot in life."

Regarding this view of responsibility, Sobottka goes on to say, "This is seemingly an empowering concept, because it requires that we accept the responsibility of being the sole cause of our destiny. However, a danger is that it can lead to tremendous guilt, regret, and self-condemnation when the inevitable misfortunes and disasters occur and we are forced to accept that our own choices brought them about. The only way out of this guilt is to realize that we also have the choice of whether or not to feel guilty, and to regard the event as a blessing rather than a disaster."

Free Will vs. Determinism

I experienced something like this when I went to my family doctor for what I thought was a simple but aggravating itch on my arms and legs, and after myriad tests, over a period of several months, was diagnosed with an incurable, progressive, liver disease. I did *not* see that coming. The stresses of the life I was living as a small business owner working sixty hours a week had taken a lot out of me and I was on the mat.

For the first time in my life I felt truly helpless. Having always enjoyed excellent health and a lean, strong body, I had taken my health for granted and never had much cause to question my physical capabilities. Now I faced a medical condition with a frightening prognosis. I had survived Vietnam unscathed, how could I possibly be facing a life of permanent disability?

In *"You Can Heal Your Life"* by Louise Hay I read that anger is the emotional expression that manifests in the body as liver problems. She had pointed out the direct connection between the mind and body, and once I started thinking about anger I could see anger everywhere; I just never realized how truly angry I was, but I was angry, really angry. I was angry about working at a business in which I had very little interest. I was angry about being uncomfortable with my life. I was angry about what was going on in Washington; I was even angry about ABC changing programming on Thursdays.

I came to realize that all I had to do was stop being angry, and that the other side of this *disability* was the *ability*, and the opportunity, for me to write at my own pace. It was an invitation to reconnect with the creative me that had gotten splintered off somewhere along the way. I realized that the illness I was facing was, for me, a way out of the stressful life that I had created.

This way of thinking comes from a position of duality. There was self and other, good and bad, freedom and responsibility, all in the context of determinism. In duality, I believed that taking responsibility for the emotional basis of the disease and making a conscious effort to not be angry improved my condition. Duality is where free will and determinism, along with all other polarities, do battle in our hearts, and minds, and our souls. For all this, we are responsible.

Responsibility doesn't look quite the same from the nondual perspective. Later in the same chapter, Sobottka expands on the nondual view of responsibility, or lack thereof. "If there is no responsibility, what is to prevent an individual from being irresponsible, perhaps even indulging in the desire to steal or murder? If stealing or murder is to occur, then it will occur, if not, it won't. This will be true both before and after a person questions the concept of responsibility. Everything happens as it must, whether or not the concept of responsibility exists. It is very clear that the concept of responsibility has not prevented stealing and murder from happening in the past. Everything is part of the impersonal functioning of Consciousness, including stealing and murder. In addition to producing suffering, the concept of responsibility encourages a sense of moral outrage to arise when the event occurs, and a sense of moral retribution when the 'perpetrator' has been caught and punished. Both reinforce the concept of separation. Of course, there is no perpetrator. We must clearly understand, however, that the widespread beliefs in the concepts of responsibility and retribution are also merely part of the functioning of Consciousness. It is all happening just as it must."

Trying to understand nonduality in terms of concepts frequently appears paradoxical to the mind. Sobottka explains how the subject of free will is handled by different nondual teachers. "The sense of being a separate individual is necessarily associated with the concomitant sense of having free will. Therefore, as long as we think of ourselves as individuals, we will feel that we are making choices. Some sages capitalize on this by teaching us that we are free to enquire into this sense of individuality and free will and thereby to look for the source of the I-notion. But freedom of choice can only be a concept that may be useful for some people at some time to encourage them to question their freedom of choice and to see whether there can be true freedom in a mere concept.

"From this discussion, we can see that to question the existence of free will is only one approach to the problem. Another approach is to question the existence of the I-entity itself." From a nondual perspective, there is neither free will nor responsibility since there is no individuality to express either. In duality, where we live, there appears to be both free will and responsibility, operating in a deterministic universe.

Moral Foundations

The individual perspective, in conjunction with whatever is other, uses the conviction of owning responsibility to fortify its position as a separate entity and master of its own fate. It is from this profound certainty that *we must be individuals* that the problem of free will arises. In the face of powerful arguments that we cannot possibly be morally responsible in the ultimate way that we think we are, come equally compelling psychological and social motivations why we must continue to believe that we are, in the final analysis, morally responsible individuals.

Whether or not free will exists has ceased to be the issue, for it is now a matter of survival; not just survival of the individual and the hope of finding any purpose or sense of personal accomplishment in life, but also the survival of civilization as we know it, for moral responsibility is at the root of all we are taught to believe.

The consensus of Western belief, it seems, is that if it weren't for our sense of moral responsibility, as guided, either directly or indirectly, by some particular brand of exoteric Western religion, the world would surely be going straight to hell, and that without individuality, humankind would simply cease to exist. Is this true, or is it an illusion? Are both free will and determinism just ideas that guide the structure of our thinking? Sophia knows.

*"The most beautiful as well as the most ugly inclinations of man
are not part of a fixed biologically given human nature,
but result from the social process which creates man."*

Erich Fromm

Processes

"A child of five would understand this.
Send someone to fetch a child of five."

Groucho Marx

Chapter Eight

A Child's Garden

The story of Adam and Eve in the Garden of Eden was one of the first Bible stories I recall hearing as a child. Most everyone brought up in any Western culture has heard this story from the Old Testament, which is the one holy book accepted by Judaism, Christianity and Islam. As a child, I was told what it meant for Adam and Eve, and, more significantly, what it meant for the rest of us. This is where it stopped making sense to me; as a child of five or so, I was unable to make the connection between what Adam and Eve had done and the idea of original sin. Taken as a statement of fact, as children are inclined to do, original sin didn't ring true; I learned that sin was something you did that was wrong. To the mind of this curious child, I did not understand how someone who hasn't done anything could have done something wrong, how could it possibly be wrong to be born?

Joseph Campbell, in *Thou Art That*, explains how this story began. "The first part of the book of Genesis is sheer mythology, and it is largely that of the Mesopotamian people. Here we have the Garden of Eden, for this is the mythological age in which we enter a mythological garden. The story of not eating the apple of the forbidden tree is an old folklore motif that is called 'the one forbidden thing.' Do not open this door, do not look over here, do not eat this food. If you want to understand why God would have done a thing like that, all you need do is tell somebody, 'Don't do this.' Human nature will do the rest.

"God's idea, in this story, was to get Adam and Eve out of that Garden. What was it about the Garden? It was a place of oneness, of unity, of no divisions in the nature of people or things. When you eat the Fruit of the Knowledge of Good and Evil, however, you know about pairs of opposites, which include not only good and evil, light and dark, right and wrong, but male and female, and God and Man as well." Campbell goes on to point out how religion has assumed "that God exiled Adam and Eve from the Garden, but actually they exiled themselves. This story yields its meaning only to a psychological interpretation. If you explain it as an historical event that occurred at some distant time back there, it seems ridiculous. There was no Garden of Eden as a concrete place. To believe so is to misunderstand and misconstrue the metaphoric language of religion."

Religious Education

Yet this is exactly what we do when we try to teach religious ideas to children who can only understand them as history or science. The story never has a chance to deliver its mythological message because it is never understood as a myth. It is imperative that we weigh the consequences of indoctrinating our children into a system of beliefs that is at odds with the rational thinking that is responsible for the structure of the technological and scientific culture in which we live.

In his book *god is not Great: How Religion Poisons Everything*, Christopher Hitchens devotes an entire chapter to the question, *Is Religion Child Abuse?* The issue opens on the jacket flap where we find, "'God did not make us,' he writes, 'We made God.' Religion, he explains, is a distortion of our origins, our nature, and the cosmos. We damage our children – and endanger our world – by indoctrinating them." The idea of religious child abuse must certainly include recent reports of physical sexual encounters between clergymen and their young charges, but it must also include what children are taught and how they are taught in a religious setting. Private schools adhere to different standards with regard to curriculum and student rights than do public, government supported schools. Tales of corporal punishment in Catholic Parochial schools are the stuff of urban legends.

The curriculum includes religious education, of course, which is accepted by most children as truth at the same level as reading, writing, and 'rithmetic. In his book, Hitchens retells a story by author, Mary McCarthy. "In her *Memories of a Catholic Girlhood,* Mary McCarthy remembers her shock at learning from a Jesuit preacher that her Protestant grandfather – her guardian and friend – was doomed to eternal punishment because he had been baptized in the wrong way. A precociously intelligent child, she would not let the matter drop until she had made the Mother Superior consult some higher authorities and discover a loophole in the writings of Bishop Athanasius, who held that heretics were only damned if they rejected the true church with full awareness of what they were doing. Her grandfather, then, might be sufficiently unaware of the true church to evade hell. But what an agony to which to subject an eleven year-old girl! And only think of the number of less curious children who simply accepted this evil teaching without questioning it. Those who lie to the young in this way are wicked in the extreme."

While Hitchens is a devout atheist, Paul Alan Laughlin, who is a Christian minister, leans in a similar direction when he writes in *Remedial Christianity* of the long-term effects of teaching the doctrine of original sin. "Although no expert on child-rearing, I am convinced that if children are constantly told that they are evil and worthless, there is a good chance that they will become adults who are precisely that. Conversely, if children are reared with a positive sense of their basic goodness and worth, they will become reasonably healthy adults with wholesome self-images and strong self-esteem. In this regard, there is cause to worry about a religion whose basic view of humanity is that in its natural state it is a 'mass of damnation' corrupted by sin, powerless to do good 'under its own steam,' and bound for hell. Especially in contrast with Eastern faiths, which not only have no strong doctrine of sin but actually begin with a premise of everyone's essential divinity. Original sin seems a formidably debilitating doctrine." I remind you that the idea of original sin was not taught by Jesus, but developed around the story of the Garden of Eden, primarily in the teachings of St. Augustine.

A child has no ability to discriminate between the symbolism of a myth and a story as history. Yet we are exposed to these teachings at an age when we cannot understand symbolism and we do in fact think of them as history. As children we desperately want the world to make sense and we want to trust those who care for and teach us. However, even as adults who have gained knowledge of the world and understand the concept of myth, a significant number of people continue to think of these myths as true in an historical sense.

A sensible approach to spiritual education might be to teach children about all of the major paths, what each believes, how they practice, and what they offer as benefits, then to let the child choose which path it will follow, if any at all. The catch is that a significant part of the doctrine of Western religion calls for a spiritual imperialism that compels true believers to impose their beliefs on others, so that everyone might be saved. In this light, it would be spiritually irresponsible for parents who believe the doctrine, not to share these beliefs with their children.

Hitchens reflects on this issue; "If religious instruction were not allowed until the child had attained the age of reason, we would be living in a quite different world. Faithful parents are divided over this, since they naturally hope to share the wonders and delights of Christmas and other fiestas with their offspring (and can also make good use of god, as well as of lesser figures like Santa Claus, to help tame the unruly) but mark what happens if the child should stray to another faith, let alone another cult, even in early adolescence. The parents will tend to proclaim that this is taking advantage of the in-nocent. All monotheisms have, or used to have, a very strong prohibi-tion against apostasy for just this reason."

If events continue unfolding in the present pattern, this situation is not likely to improve anytime soon, as Western religion shapes the standards for powerful cultural, governmental, and economic forces, and these are the standards that we will pass on to our children, both Christian and Muslim. They will learn that what they are taught to believe *is* true and that anyone who does not believe this, is wrong and possibly evil. We will teach them that their ideology is worth dying for, and moreover worth killing for. We teach them daily in the news of the world.

There is a long history of conflict between these two belief systems and little hope for a lasting resolution. Many died during the Crusades when weapons were primitive and war was an intimate affair. Since the Cold War of the mid twentieth century, however, children have learned to live with the threat of a war such as has never been seen before. For my generation, it would be a bomb from the sky, there would be warning to find shelter, those who did not find shelter would likely be killed immediately, and life for the survivors would be a living hell. For children today, danger is everywhere, there is no warning, there is no escape, there is no defense; in an instant, everything could be over, no more world. This is part of what we teach them and this is what they believe.

Graphic Imagery

Children think primarily in images and a child will construct a mental image in order to comprehend something. What must be the image in the child's mind of a God who evicts his children from the Garden of Eden because they were duped by another of God's creatures, and then curses all of their descendents for that alleged misdeed? What face could a child put on a God who demanded that Abraham kill his own son and then at the eleventh hour retracted that demand and called it a test of Abraham's faith? How does a young mind picture a God who murdered every first-born child in Egypt because the Pharaoh would not free the Hebrew slaves? How could a child see a God who killed every living thing in a flood, except for Noah and his family and two of each animal? (although I always thought that most of the fish were probably okay) When viewed in terms of what modern religion teaches as morality, the God of Abraham and Moses behaved very badly.

In the New Testament, there is a striking contrast between the gentle teachings of Jesus and the atrocities associated with the God of the Old Testament. The Old Testament image of God as the all powerful absolute ruler who demands blind obedience and severely punishes those who deviate, is transformed after the birth of Jesus and we are introduced to an image of God as a benevolent father figure who loves his creation and wants us all to go to Heaven to be with Him for eternity. So much did God love the world, I was told repeatedly and with great conviction, that He gave His only begotten Son that we might be forgiven for original sin. I didn't get it; Jesus seemed like a really good guy and he was God's Son, so why did God kill him?

Yet this is what I was told, that we must believe that Jesus was the Son of God who died for our sins in order that we can be saved and go to Heaven; otherwise, according to what I was taught to believe in a Christian home, we are all going to Hell. Though I eventually came to understand the symbolism behind the idea of original sin, I have yet to make the connection between Jesus dying on the cross and those who believe in Him going to Heaven.

Many childish questions arose regarding the subject of Hell: Who goes to Hell? What about the people who lived and died before Jesus came to save them? What becomes of the millions of Hindus and Buddhists who were not able to know of the existence of Jesus? Jesus was Jewish not Christian, what of the Jews, His chosen people? How could a God of love and justice sentence a large segment of humanity to eternity in Hell for not following a path that was not available to them? Why even bother to bring these poor doomed souls into the world?

Omnipotence, Omniscience, and Omnipresence

Another aspect of the Christian teaching presented to me as a child was that God was all powerful, all knowing, and everywhere at once. This was not easy for a young mind to digest and in response to this declaration; several more questions arose that have yet to be adequately addressed. How can an all powerful God be disobeyed? How can an all-knowing God not know what is going to happen in the future? If God knows the future, how can we be responsible for what happens in our lives? If God is everywhere at once, is not everything part of God? If everything is part of God, are we not all part of God? If we are part of God, how can anything we do possibly be wrong? If God, who is also touted as being ultimate goodness, is all these things, then a child has to ask why is there evil at all?

We discussed *The Problem of Good and Evil* in Chapter 6, but the real problem is much larger than the duality of *Good vs. Evil*. The nature of duality presents a world and a mode of thinking that only recognizes self and other. This creates a situation where we feel we are competing with all that is other for limited resources, and control becomes a very important aspect of life.

Control Issues

In Western culture, while we have learned a certain appreciation for the beauty of nature, we are also taught that both the nature of the earth and our own human nature are to be feared. Today, many people are concerned with the state of the environment and what is in store for future generations. On a daily basis, deadly storms, earthquakes and various microbes threaten our existence, as do asteroids, comets, and the very sun that gives us life. From the inside, our lives are endangered by what have been called the seven deadly sins, (pride, greed, envy, gluttony, anger, sloth, and lust) which create social conflicts that usually result in great suffering.

Absolute power, knowledge, and presence represent the ultimate control. If humanity cannot control its circumstances, and when faced with the awesome power of nature we surely cannot, then we seem directed to believe that such control must exist in the hands of some benevolent deity who supports our existence. Such a God would not only be the Creator of the universe, but would also be the mightiest King of that creation. He would impose rules and make judgments, but He would protect the faithful and obedient, for they would have God on their side. The perfect God would display all the virtues of an idealized human, but have ultimate control over everything including nature. Thus, we have the image of the wise and powerful grandfather figure with a long flowing beard, sitting on a throne in the sky. When the child's mind tries to grasp the Absolute it must define it as something, but I wondered how the source of everything can be any kind of something?

Lies, Deceptions, and Platitudes

The unanswerable questions continued to roll from my young mind like an annoying two year old who keeps asking "why" to every answer given. Because someone told me to have faith was not a reasonable argument, and reason was my guide. I wanted the truth and I saw no cause to believe that anyone I knew as a child had the slightest idea what truth was. Then, when I was only seven years old, something occurred that eliminated any possibility that I could ever believe the teachings of Christianity. Perhaps I was more sensitive than my peers who cast off this common childhood deception as a rite of passage, but for me it was a matter of trust.

I heard rumors that there was no Santa Claus, and a few weeks later on the night of Christmas Eve I went to bed when told to do so and stayed quiet until everyone else was asleep; I then came downstairs to wait in vain for Santa to arrive. I remained awake at my post until sunrise and awoke from a light sleep at the base of the Christmas tree when my mother entered the room in the morning carrying presents to put under the tree. My mother had always told me that the one thing she would not tolerate was lying, but she had lied to me, and it wasn't just her, it was a conspiracy as large as the religion itself.

My superficial reaction was disappointment that Santa Claus was not "real" but the effect went far beyond disenchantment with this particular myth. Upon reflection, I had to consider that if my mother, who otherwise seemed to be a rational person, would lie about something this trivial, maybe there was something wrong with the big picture. What if Christianity was as a much a lie as the story of Santa? What if the Church was fooling the adults the same way the adults were fooling the children? The larger question was, what if God, if indeed there was a God, was fooling the Church the same way the adults were fooling the children? I also had to consider the possibility that they were all fooling themselves just because religion made them feel better.

Both Christmas and Easter, the two major Christian holidays, have become secularized and culturally adapted to appeal to children by adding elements that have no religious significance whatsoever. This gives immediate positive reinforcement for participating in the celebration when the minds are not mature enough to understand abstractions such as salvation, heaven, and hell. The ideas of gifts, games, food and fun are appealing to adults as well, but these aspects of the holy days seem explicitly designed to attract children. Kids enjoy Christmas because kids like getting presents, and all the other accoutrements of the holidays. As a child who was the target of this effort, it was never quite clear to me, however, why I was getting presents on Jesus' birthday.

Some Resolution

After a lifetime of seeking truth, I believe that I understand most of the tenants of Christianity as they were intended to be understood, as mythology. In my nondualistic view of the Garden of Eden story, the forbidden fruit of the tree of the knowledge of good and evil represents the polarities that are created when judgments (as to good and evil) take place. Adam and Eve, representing our species, made the first judgment and in so doing, they banished themselves from paradise by separating themselves from the Oneness, which, unlike the God of exoteric religion, does not judge. They established a life based on judgment and taught it to their children who were condemned (not by God, but by the power of their own judgment) to follow in the footsteps of their parents. Sophia will tell you simply that because there is only One, there is no one to follow.

Most responses to my childish questions came as condescending platitudes; have faith they said. Ultimately, faith was what it all came down to, and questioning faith was taboo; but even as a child, I saw faith as a feeble substitute for knowledge. I also believe that many other children have questions such as the ones I have asked here from the memories of my youth and on behalf of my own inner child. Children want to believe what we teach them; they are human and need structure like any other human. The curious natural mind of the child is not sinful, but is taught to believe that in a sense, it is cursed by God. Most children accept what they are taught, and move on to other things that are more fun or required activities such as play or school, and religious ideas are accepted with little examination.

When we ask a child to believe the doctrines of Western religion, we invite confusion into their lives by giving them an ancient philosophy from the early Middle Ages or before, then asking them to believe it without question, under the threat of spending forever in the worst place imaginable – hell. The child in me had to ask why God would give us these wonderful minds if not to question, engage, discover, explore, and perhaps even understand the divine reality?

Laughlin completes this thought at the end of *Remedial Christianity* with, "It is much more reasonable to believe that such a God would be disappointed if we failed to appreciate and utilize our great gift of intellect with all our might and for whatever time is available to us. If this volume has succeeded at all in arousing in the reader the spirit of inquiry and encouraging the use of the mind with respect to her or his faith, it has served its purpose." To that I can only add, Amen.

"The real voyage of discovery
consists not in seeking new landscapes,
but in having new eyes."

Marcel Proust

Chapter Nine

Seeking Truth

Humans are social creatures and as such tend to congregate based on heredity, proximity, language, race, common beliefs about the world, and common goals. As children we learn what we live, absorbing our environment to forge our own personality, and for the most part we accept what we are told and learn what we are taught. Spiritually speaking, most people simply follow the religion of their heritage and do not actually choose a spiritual path to guide the unfolding of their lives. For these people, spirituality is usually expressed through exoteric religion, and it tells them that life has rules, structure, and meaning. Religion sanctions and binds procreative relationships; it gives comfort in times of need. By congregating with like minds, these beliefs help form a group consciousness that strengthens the individual identity to the extent that the individual relates to the values of the group.

Much of what is passed down through generations, such as thoughts relating to science and technology, are subject to a progressive kind of learning that can easily be changed based on new knowledge and experience. Some thoughts, the idea of family for instance, can be integral to cultural norms, and therefore resistant to change, even when there may be good reasons to change those thoughts. For many people, however, religion alone stands completely outside of reason, as it is self-validating and creates its own context in which it is beyond reproach.

Religion as a Belief System

In his book, *Breaking the Spell*, Daniel Dennett discusses how religion might have evolved, in a Darwinian sense, not within our genes, but within our culture. As with biological evolution, cultural evolution must have a benefit to the cause of self-replication. In this case, it must have a benefit to the culture and also a benefit to the individuals, as it is the individuals who form and perpetuate the culture. Dennett cites the following three cultural benefits or purposes of religion as evolutionary advantages:

1.) "to *comfort* us in our suffering and allay our fear of death,

2.) "to *explain* things we can't otherwise explain," and

3.) "to encourage group *cooperation* in the face of trials and enemies."

When religious doctrine was canonized, these were major issues for the people of that time, as they are for people today. Death has always been, and likely will always be, a problem for individuals who know that inevitably they will die. While religion continues to offer comfort to the righteous with the promise of life eternal, its authority to effectively explain the mysterious has been usurped by the rational approach that science has taken to understanding our world. The type of group cooperation elicited by religion depends on identification with the in-group, but duality requires that if there is an in-group there must also be an out-group, which makes every other group wrong and a potential enemy. Intra-group cooperation may be enhanced by religion, but inter-group cooperation is restricted by the "believe this or be damned" attitude that dominates Western religious thought.

In our modern world, religious claims, by aspiring to factual status, weaken their credibility in the face of logic and reason. Though some efforts have been made to update the dogma, most religions were designed to address the consciousness of another time, and Western religions have left little wiggle room by playing "the inerrant Word of

God" card. Religion, by claiming to be an expression of fact, as stated by none other than God Himself, has painted itself into a corner to the degree that a truly effective modernization could necessitate a rewriting of the entire system. Applying our currently preferred mode of scientific thinking, if we understand religion as a myth, the world devalues it as not factual, but if we try to understand it as fact, it is difficult not to consider it nonsense.

Our pursuit of understanding the world through science has certainly left religion wanting for credibility. In *The Wisdom of Insecurity* Alan Watts wrote, "What science has said, in sum, is this: We do not, and in all probability cannot, know whether God exists. Nothing that we do know suggests that he does, and all the arguments which claim to prove his existence are found to be without logical meaning." True believers, however, do not seem terribly bothered by logical arguments and compartmentalize their thinking to avoid collisions between their knowledge and their beliefs.

Optional and Auxiliary Belief Systems

Others have sublimated some of the energy of spiritual seeking into pursuits they consider more practical; power and wealth are particularly prominent at this time. However, whether one is driven by a quest for enlightenment or to have a greater net worth than Bill Gates makes little difference as far as the individual is concerned, the objective is always validation and enhancement of the ego. One who is on a so called "spiritual" path may look down on those who seek their truth in the world of high finance as being materialistic, but both are paths in duality. Piety and self-righteousness aside, trying to become a better individual, by any means and to whatever end, is seeking ego gratification in duality.

One can seek the ultimate truth in any venue, but the traditional paths in Western culture are; philosophy, religion, science, social science, and more recently, what have become known as New Age teachings. Spiritual seekers are those who are in search of something beyond the mainstream spiritual experience and are usually willing to break with tradition to find it. How "something beyond" is defined will vary from case to case and may even be admittedly unknown. Desire drives seeking and one can desire anything one can conceptualize. In this chapter, we will focus on the seeking of what we believe to be spiritual or at least higher truth.

There have always been seekers of spiritual truth, but for much of our history, going against the grain of the established system of beliefs could be fatal. This situation improved greatly beginning with the Renaissance and continuing through the Philosophical Enlightenment of the eighteenth century. In the mid twentieth century a cascade of social factors united to launch a cultural revolution that quickly spread throughout Western civilization when the post World War II baby boom demographic was entering adolescence in the early 1960's.

This revolution was in response to the rigidity of post WWII society, the oppression of women and various minorities, and the restrictive moral codes that had grown out of Western religion. At the center of all this was a shift of consciousness that first had to shake off the old ways before moving forward. Political and anti-war factions played an important role in opposing the status quo, as did the arts, especially popular music. Psychedelic drugs and free love were on the list of mind-expanding options available to those willing to reach beyond the behavioral norms of their parents. Though the success of the revolution at overthrowing the existing culture, was limited at best, in many ways this period profoundly influenced the way we live today.

As the rebellious boomers matured into a more conventional adulthood, the radical nature of the counterculture morphed into a more spiritual movement that we know today as the New Age. In addition to the wide variety of new teachings that became available, the blossoming of the New Age has revived many traditional teachings, not only from the East, but from the pagan traditions of Europe as well. Buddhism, Taoism, and certain sects of Hinduism are gaining practitioners in the West, but the Wiccan, Gnostic, and Druid belief systems are also staging a comeback. In addition to the various revivals, there are numerous revisions that have been dubbed "Neo" traditions. Most every teaching from Advaita Vedanta to Zoroastrianism has been neo-ized and adapted by the New Age movement to fit better into modern Western culture.

Meditation

Meditation, in some form, seems to be an integral part of many spiritual paths, and this is not just the New Age and Eastern teachings, it is part of everyday life in the monasteries and mystery schools of Western religions. Many people start meditation and other spiritual practices as intentional efforts directed at some spiritual goal, which permits us to define meditation as productive activity. It is difficult for the mind to stay in the present moment because the present moment has no purpose, so the mind creates a purpose in the future. If your purpose in meditating is to attain enlightenment, which can only occur in the present moment, then the more valuable use of meditation might be to calm the mind rather than focus attention on a future goal.

As mentioned earlier, Zen is an Indo-European word based on the Japanese pronunciation of the Chinese word *Chan*, which means *meditation*. Many consider Zen the highest form of meditation, and in my experience, the main purpose of this type of meditation is to calm the turbulent waters of the mind by bringing attention gently into the present moment. According to the Britannica Concise Encyclopedia, during Zen meditation "Logical, analytic thinking is suspended, as are all desires, attachments, and judgments, leaving the mind in a state of relaxed attention." When the mind is truly calm and unattached, duality becomes remarkably transparent.

The Sincerest Form of Flattery

I'm sure that when I was a member of Eckankar the following idea was never part of the formal teaching, but I do remember much talk of this particular approach to spirituality, which I like to call the *fake it 'til you make it* school of thought. I have encountered this attitude often in people of diverse backgrounds and belief systems. (What would Jesus do?) The psychological position of these seekers is to try to imitate the attributes that they believe represent the expression of enlightenment, or at least a "higher" spiritual position than they will claim for them-selves, such as being calm and detached.

As superficial as this approach may seem, I believe that it could facilitate movement toward enlightenment. It can help calm the mind and make possible a degree of detachment. The main danger that I see in this approach is that the seeker's mind has to interpret these overt behaviors and deduce the perspective from which the behaviors emanate. Because the mind observes only the outward behavior and cannot understand the conditions at the root of these appearances, it may project the appearance of *calmness* by repressing emotions, or the appearance of *detachment* might be the expression of apathy or lack of compassion for others; under such conditions difficulties are likely to arise. Possibly a worse outcome would be the ego who mastered the outward appearances of enlightenment and believed itself to be enlightened. Deeply delusional egos can be powerful magnets attracting those who yearn for leadership.

Fundamentalism as a Trend

In her bestseller, *The Battle for God*, Karen Armstrong tracks the emergence of fundamentalism in the evolution (if I may use that word) of Western exoteric religion. Over the past 250 years or so, religion survived various divisions, the Philosophical Enlightenment, intellectual rationalism, the industrial revolution, secular education, and finally, World War II. While the observance of religious services remained, in many communities, a nearly mandatory social function, many began to look for sturdier things on which to lean. Armstrong notes that, "In the early twentieth century, people were trying to find new ways to be religious." Science spoke a clear truth and, in time became the main support of Western culture. Some, however, chose to restore the finality of the path by insisting on a literal interpretation of the scripture.

We have talked about the nature of fundamentalism elsewhere in the book, but the fact that it is gaining popularity leaves the future looking somewhat precarious as nations with nuclear weapons play *My God is better than your God*. In her book, *The Battle for God*, Armstrong offers a detailed historical analysis of how things came to this point, and expresses concern about the direction the fundamentalist movement may be taking. Related issues are brought to light in *The End of Faith*, another bestseller by Sam Harris, who points out that while the extremists are bad, the existence of moderates who are obliged to accept the ideas of the extremists because they believe the same basic tenants, make the situation even more volatile. In the first chapter, he cites religious tolerance as a major obstacle to resolving the problems that come with fundamentalism, and defines one purpose of his book. "I hope to show that the very ideal of religious tolerance – born of the notion that every human being should be free to believe whatever he wants about God – is one of the principal forces driving us toward the abyss." Dangerous extremists hide in the religious tolerance of others, but offer no such consideration in return. Fundamentalist Western religions do not foresee world peace until only one religion remains – theirs. They can only accept peace in terms of their own teaching, for that is what the teachings of Christianity and Islam require when taken literally.

Attracting the Good Life

On a brighter note, a group of teachings have emerged in the last decade or so that I would consider a hybrid of higher spirituality and personal motivation. Probably the best-known advocates of this path are Esther and Jerry Hicks, who wrote what has become a very popular book titled *Ask and It Is Given*. The substance of the book, and the many others that have followed, is communications from a group of nonphysical entities channeling through Esther's voice. The entities go by the name *Abraham* and their teaching says that we, as individuals, can have whatever we want if we approach it in the right way. I think of this as the *get what you want* school of thought. The essence of the teaching is that reality is the result of conscious creation and operates by the Law of Attraction. On their introductory presentation, which is available as a free audio recording on their website, Abraham speaks through Esther addressing the Law of Attraction.

In the recording, Abraham states that The Law of Attraction, which is summarized as "That which is like unto itself is drawn," is the most powerful law in the universe. They emphasize the importance of what we think and say by asserting that those who speak of illness attract illness into their lives, and that those who speak of prosperity are, or will become, prosperous. Attention is likened to a magnet that attracts that about which you think and feel. If you give attention to feeling fat, you will not lose weight, and if you feel poor you will not become wealthy.

First you must understand that you attract what you *think* about, then you begin to pay attention to *what* you are thinking. In this view we are the creators of our experience and we do so through thought, word, and action. When the question arises, "Why do I experience that which I do not want in my life?" we are told that we are creating by default because we are misunderstanding the rules of the game.

The rules are simple: you create your experience by what you think and talk about, and by what you do. When you think about what you <u>do not</u> want rather than what you <u>do</u> want, then what you <u>do not</u> want is attracted into your life. The Law of Attraction gives our attention the power to create your experience. In duality, this is true; but it is not quite as simple as it appears. The major difficulty that I see with this approach is in the assumption that *what we want* and *what we think about* are matters of volition. In each of us there is a lifetime of experience that has shaped our fears and our desires. Preconceived notions define our ideas of good and bad, of what is desirable and what is not. In almost every case, what we want is to enhance the ego in some way.

While instant results are not necessarily to be expected, the claim is clearly stated that focusing attention on what you want will bring it to you, "and if you stay focused upon it long enough, it absolutely, under all conditions, will be yours, you see."

Another essential part of this teaching is called the Law of Deliberate Creation. In this law, as implied above, creation is not optional, for thoughts are creative by nature, and rarely are humans at a loss for thoughts. The deliberate part comes as a matter of choice and is crucial to this teaching. Human beings think almost constantly and these thoughts have consequences in the physical state, not only in the present, but also by implication into the future. The Law of Attraction works whether you are thinking about something you want or some-thing you do not want, so a big part of this practice is deciding what you want and thinking about it. The challenge that is often encountered comes in deciding what you *really* want. With crossed purposes, conflicting desires and various other influences, "What do you want?" is a very complicated question. What we want, however, may not be as important as what we expect. Due to the influences of genetics, culture, relationships, and conditioning of all sorts, desires and expectations are sometimes in opposition to each other. It will be a much harder road if our expectations stand in the way of our desires.

What really makes this system work is the Law of Allowing, through which our desires are manifested into reality. This law is the basis for accepting the current state of affairs in life as the natural result of thoughts and conditioning in the past. When employing the Law of Allowing properly, there will be this accepting of others as well, as we understand that their circumstances are also the result of thoughts and conditioning. The Law of Allowing is accepting *what is* and not being in conflict with life in the present moment.

This path presents some fascinating considerations. In the Law of Attraction, I see the idea that we are connected to our environment which alludes to a sense of unity. The Law of Allowing hints at the disillusion of the ego and invites us to rise above our conditioning by reducing our tendency to judge people and events in negative ways. This approach heightens the awareness that we are one with our perceptions and our world, teaches unconditional acceptance of *what is*, and directs the ego to view reality as the result of natural processes rather than as a foe to be conquered.

This teaching has grown into a movement with many teachers from varied backgrounds using these same "laws" as tools for everything from personal motivational coaching to approaches that appear much more spiritual. Any path is going to attract a lot of interest when it says to the ego, "You can have what you want by focusing on what you want rather than focusing on what you don't want, as long as you are able to suspend negative judgments regarding whatever is reality in the present." It sounds relatively easy, because we believe our thoughts and desires are the product of free will; if we choose our thoughts and if our thoughts control reality, we really must be capable of changing life for the *better*. Better, of course, is defined by the same conditioned ego that is expressing the desire.

The Adventures of Joe

While many have taken up the banner of the Law of Attraction, with a doctorate degree in Metaphysical Science and another doctorate in Marketing, author Joe Vitale was perfect to pick up on the Abraham teachings. Vitale is charismatic, smart, ambitions, and very successful, with widely varied interests and investments. As he grew in his own success, Vitale recorded it all for posterity and sold it to the world. He has written many books, mostly about how to make lots of money in a short amount of time (read as "get rich quick" if you like), including two time international bestseller, *The Attractor Factor: 5 Easy steps for Creating Wealth (and anything else) from the inside out*, which was based on the Law of Attraction as described in the teachings of Abraham.

Vitale's more recent effort takes us down a different road. Through his friend Ihaleakala Hew Len, Vitale learned Ho'oponopono, the Hawaiian healing method. His book, *Zero Limits: The Secret Hawaiian System for Wealth, Health, Peace and More*, which became an Amazon.com bestseller before it was released, is about Vitale's experience with this method of healing, and is co-authored by Hew Len.

Back in the 1980's, Hew Len, a psychologist, learned the technique from Morrnah Simeona who had revised and updated what is believed to be an ancient Hawaiian teaching. Using this method, Hew Len reportedly healed an entire ward of criminally insane people at the Hawaiian State Hospital. Most of the information reported in this book came from a website, www.hooponopono.org, which was closed for a while but, at the time of this writing, has reopened. There is an article on the site by Hew Len consisting of fourteen, disjointed, mostly short, dated entries beginning in January of 2005, and spread out over the following thirteen months. The article is loosely structured and broad in its approach: it quotes Paul Simon, Shakespeare, Jesus, and others; it cites academic research including that of Benjamin Libet, whose work we discussed in the chapter on Free Will. The article contains tables and flowcharts; it tells stories that serve as testimonials; he makes a wide variety of bold statements, some of which I found unmistakably profound, some I thought rationally questionable.

It is often difficult to understand new ideas unless they can be positioned properly within our normal thinking framework. I believe Hew Len's intention in this article was to offer a *shotgun* approach presenting the underlying principles of Ho'oponopono in a variety of formats, perhaps in hopes that the reader will resonate with enough of it to pursue the teaching more in depth. In addition, when we speak of anything we speak from the culture in which we were raised, and the same applies when we listen. I know very little about the native Hawaiian culture, and in this sense there is a gap that some can cross more readily than I can. As already noted, I have difficulty absorbing teachings based on cultures other than the one in which I was raised; so, I read Vitale's book in order to get a more mainstream American cultural perspective on Ho'oponopono.

In the first chapter he quotes a definition that he and a friend found on the web site for hooponopono.org; "Ho'oponopono is a process of letting go of toxic energies within you to allow the impact of Divine thoughts, words, deeds, and actions." They found this curious, but it raised more questions than it answered. Continuing the investigation they learned of an updated version of the teaching, sort of a Neo-Ho'oponopono, that was called *Self I-Dentity through Ho'oponopono (SITH)*. Searching further, they found another article relating to using SITH in a psychotherapeutic setting. The article took an extreme view regarding the responsibility of the therapist in dealing with clients.

"To be an effective problem solver, the therapist must be willing to be 100 percent responsible for having created the problem situation; that is, he must be willing to see that the source of the problem is erroneous thoughts within him, not within the client. Therapists never seem to notice that every time there is a problem, they are always present!"

Joe was intrigued, but many questions remained, so the investigation continued. Other articles contributed useful information such as, "Self I-Dentity through Ho'oponopono sees each problem not as an ordeal, but as an opportunity. Problems are just replayed memories of the past showing up to give us one more chance to see with the eyes of LOVE and to act from inspiration." Finding little information that effectively and concisely described Ho'oponopono and how it works; they decided to contact Hew Len directly to get the real story. After some e-mail correspondence, they arranged a meeting in conjunction with a seminar that Hew Len was giving in Los Angeles.

The presentation began with Hew Len speaking on the persistence of memories, explaining that, "What you want to do is erase them completely and permanently." Taken in isolation, and from my cultural perspective, that statement sounds patently absurd, as it literally advocates total amnesia. What I think he is really addressing is not a problem with the memories themselves, but the strife that can result from defining the present in terms of those memories. This is especially true with memories buried deep in the unconscious where their influence manifests powerfully in our daily lives, but goes virtually unnoticed by the conscious mind. In Hew Len's view, we live our lives either from these memories, or from what he calls inspiration. According to him, "Inspiration is the Divine giving you a message... The only way to hear the Divine and receive inspiration is to clean all memories. The only thing you have to do is clean." Cleaning memories was another phrase I was not familiar with, but I think I understand the concept. What I think he is talking about is releasing the identification with the memories that limit and define us, and in so doing, ending the automatic responses that bind us to duality and make us slaves to the program of the ego.

Cleaning apparently takes several forms, but the most popular, and the one Joe was willing to share with his readers, is a very simple process. When you recognize that the motivation behind an action you are taking may be old habits that are based on toxic memories, you make four statements addressing the Divine;

"I love you."

"I'm sorry."

"Please forgive me."

"Thank you."

Joe did not understand how this could possibly be of any value, though he did not find the idea unappealing, after all, how could saying the words "I love you" be a problem for anyone? Hew Len addressed Joe directly from the stage during a seminar and asked him, "How do you know whether something is a memory or an inspiration?"

Joe "didn't understand the question" and said so.

"How do you know if someone who gets cancer gave it to themselves or it was given to them by the Divine as a challenge to help them?" Hew Len queried. Joe said he did not know, and Hew Len admitted that he did not know either, therefore, "You have to clean on anything and everything, as you have no idea what is memory and what is inspiration." Joe resisted this idea as his career and his life were based on the idea that controlling the mind was what made things go your way. His view started to change, however, when he read a book that recounted scientific evidence, such as that of Benjamin Libet, which does not support the validity of intention. He quotes from Libet's book about his experiments, *Mind Time*, "The unconscious appearance of an intention to act could not be controlled consciously. Only its final consummation in a motor act could be consciously controlled."

In *Hare Brain, Tortoise Mind,* by Professor of Learning Sciences, Guy Claxton, Joe read that, "No intention is ever hatched in consciousness; no plan ever laid there. Intentions are premonitions; icons that flash in the corners of consciousness to indicate what may be about to occur." These ideas rocked Joe's world as he had emphasized the power of intentions as a conscious force in shaping our lives. Joe believed that he lost 80 pounds by being mentally tough and asserting his intention to lose weight.

Hew Len introduced another new idea when he said; "You clean to get to a place of zero limits, which is the zero state." Hew Len explains the zero state as a position of neutrality, where your concerns are not weighted by memories. A similar idea appears in the teachings of Zen Buddhism where it is called Beginner's Mind or Shoshin. Hew Len brings Jesus to the issue when he says, "Jesus is purported to have said: 'Seek ye first the Kingdom (Zero) and all else will be added (Inspiration).'" Hew Len goes on to say, "Zero is the residence of you and Divinity…from where and from whom all blessings – Wealth, Health, and Peace – flow." This quote seems to have brought us back to the title of Vitale's book.

Joe eventually came to understand Ho'oponopono, at least well enough to accept it, claiming in his book, that once you start to work with it, you discover that; it is simple, easy to use, feels good, and it seems to work. Though he alludes to an enlightenment experience in the *Epilogue* of *Zero Limits*, Joe seems to me the eternal seeker, who is trying to put the pieces together much like other seekers. He does it with a great deal of flair and enthusiasm and has attracted a lot of attention in the process. Next, Joe took off on a new track that he calls the Emotional Freedom Technique or EFT, but that is another story.

The most recent news I have of Joe is his appearance in a new movie by Isaac Allen and Chad Cameron called *Leap!*, which is very much about awakening to nondual truth. Definitely worth seeing, in the movie, Vitale along with scientists, spiritual leaders, and other explorers of consciousness discuss the illusory nature of reality. Various *chapters* in the movie focus on *The Science, Perception, Illusion, Movie Metaphor, Suffering, The Ego, Happiness*, and more. The last chapter invites the viewer to *Take the Leap!*

Seeking the End of Seeking

Joe and the rest of us seek because we believe that we are the ego, and as such, we feel incomplete, inadequate, and in need of improvement, validation, and justification. We live our lives from the position of constantly seeking security in the form of something substantial, permanent, and satisfying. Some of us call that something *truth*, and that is what we claim to seek. It is the ego, however, which believes itself to be in charge of this truth seeking project, and the first thing the ego must do is to define truth. The world of the ego has nothing to do with truth, it has to do with separate things existing in space and time. Ultimately, the truth is that there is nothing to seek, and the only thing standing between you and truth is the belief that you can be separate from truth.

There is Nothing to Improve

It is in order to become a better ego, that the ego seeks anything, including enlightenment, not knowing that enlightenment is the antithesis of ego. These days, spirituality is getting all mixed up with the human potential movement or self-improvement, but enlightenment has nothing to with self-improvement as self-improvement efforts are designed to strengthen the ego. Yet, what I see in teachings such as those of Abraham or Ho'oponopono is the inclusion of nondual principles into systems that appeal strongly to a segment of the population that is more interested in empowering the egoic self than it is in enlightenment. Personally, what I thought of when first reading Abraham was that the motivational aspect of the teaching was like the tasty tidbit in which you place the large pill you have to give to your dog. Nonduality is a pill that is very difficult for the ego to swallow, but wrapping it in the promise of getting whatever the ego desires makes it a pretty easy sell. I thought it was downright ingenious to introduce nonduality into a setting where it is the essence of duality that is actually being sought. I have no way of knowing if this nondual aspect was by design or a delightful side effect.

Seeking is Life

Space does not permit a thorough coverage of the seeking process. Seeking is as large as life itself and what I have presented here in this chapter is but a small sampling of the spiritual paths available in today's world. Seeking is the ego following the impulse toward transcendence. When we look for a path, we look for one that will give us what we think we want or need. Sophia lurks in the corners of some paths and shines on the face of others.

The closing point that I will make on seeking is this; seeking happens in duality and is an expression of an egoic desire for betterment of the individual, and can be temporarily satisfied by any number of paths. To awaken, however, no path is required at all as there is nowhere to go. You have everything you need and when enlightenment occurs, you will probably be surprised to find that there no longer is anyone there to be enlightened.

"Time is too slow for those who wait,
too swift for those who fear,
too long for those who grieve,
too short for those who rejoice,
but for those who love, time is eternity."

Henry Van Dyke

Chapter Ten

It's About Time

The primary motivator of the human mind seems to be, more so than any instinct or physical drive, a need for structure. A look at any important aspect of human existence will reveal a highly structured situation. Science is perhaps the most easily recognizable example of the way knowledge has been categorized and how that structure is implemented into daily life. At the root of science is the more primary example of structure – mathematics.

Though logic and mathematics are integral to the structure of our thoughts, the logical arguments previously presented regarding free will and responsibility are not likely to change the way anyone lives, for we live a life formed primarily by perception and when information contradicts perception, perception almost always wins. As the old saying goes, "Seeing is believing."

Based on observable cycles in the environment our ancestors began making divisions in the succession of events; one rotation of the planet became a day and night, the phases of the moon mark the passing of a month, and a trip around the sun takes a year. These were powerful tools for early humans, making them able to more accurately predict nature. Today these systems have been refined and subdivided further as science has continued to advance where finer measurements seem to be required. The dividing of time may have come to an end, however, now that quantum physics has defined Plank time, which is considered the smallest measure of time in which anything can happen, as well as the measure in which everything happens.

Of more immediate importance to most people are the hours spent in support of the modern economic culture. In the context of economy I would venture to say that time is the most valuable commodity in Western culture today. We only have so much of it and we never know exactly how much that is. We even treat it like a medium of exchange; we save time, budget time, invest time, and spend time. We also speak of donating time, losing time, serving time, or wasting time. With so much of our attention focused on it, time is obviously something important, but what exactly is it?

Defining Time

The Answers.com Online Dictionary lists fourteen definitions for "time" as a noun, and several definitions for the adjective and verb forms. The broadest definition given and the one that applies best to our purpose is "a nonspatial continuum in which events occur in apparently irreversible succession from the past through the present to the future." The last part of the definition refers to the "arrow of time" which we will discuss in a moment, but what does "nonspatial continuum" mean? Nonspatial, of course, means that it doesn't incorporate or occupy space. The same website defines continuum as "a continuous extent, succession, or whole, no part of which can be distinguished from neighboring parts except by arbitrary division." That wasn't much help, all the dictionary has told us is that time is continuous and it is not space.

Most people don't really think about what time is and just accept it in the same way we accept space. While our experience tells us that time and space are very different, Einstein coined the term "spacetime" to designate the scientific union of the two ideas. Spacetime has been a prominent and accepted feature of the scientific landscape for about a hundred years, but this phenomenal discovery has not yet been incorporated into everyday thinking.

Philosopher Daniel Dennett says it this way, "When scientific advances contradict 'common sense' intuitions, the familiar ideas often linger on, not just outliving their usefulness, but even confusing the scientists whose discoveries ought to have overthrown them." Our everyday perception of time is indeed one of Dennett's "common sense intuitions," and in this world, it works. Time is one of the ways in which we structure what we perceive as reality, but because we do get quite comfortable with our mental habits, I think it is a good idea to shake things up a bit occasionally. So let's continue by taking a look at some ideas of time that might not agree with "common sense." This survey of unusual views of time will begin with the ideas behind Einstein's aforementioned term "spacetime."

Relativity and Beyond

The name Albert Einstein (1879–1955) is, in the eyes of many, synonymous with the stereotypical absent-minded genius. Einstein put a recognizable face on the stereotype of the physicist; his unruly hair and disheveled style of dress certainly made a distinctive appearance. He seemed comfortable with his fame and came across as accessible, affable and, of course, extremely intelligent. Perhaps second only to his genius, I believe what contributed most to his renown was his ability to be both precise and concise in his communications. I marvel at the power and simplicity of statements like, "Imagination is more important than knowledge," "Before God we are all equally wise—and equally foolish," "The only reason for time is so that everything doesn't happen at once." and "No problem can be solved from the same level of consciousness that created it." Even the equation that made him a legend is breathtakingly elegant and simple – $E = mc^2$.

His book, *Relativity, the Special and General Theory*, is only one hundred fifty seven pages (including five appendices) and offers "a clear explanation that anyone can understand." Unfortunately, the book includes many formulas and diagrams, which would require in depth explanations. It unfolds in such a way that specific comments on time are not easily excerpted. Fortunately, Einstein wasn't shy about speaking his marvelous mind.

The website of the American Museum of Natural History has lots of information on Einstein. Regarding his view of time amnh.org had this to say, "When Einstein proposed that the speed of light is constant for all observers, he introduced a conundrum. How could different observers measure the same speed for light when the observers themselves were moving at different speeds? Speed is a measure of distance divided by time (for example, kilometers per hour or miles per second). Einstein realized that **for speed to remain constant, intervals of time and distance would have to change** in a way that kept their ratio exactly the same.

"Einstein's answer overturned long-held ideas about the nature of time as a steady, continuous progression of events from past to present to future. Although it's hard to believe, there is no single 'master clock' for the entire universe. **Time does not progress at the same rate for everyone, everywhere.** Instead, Einstein showed that how fast time progresses depends on how fast the clock measuring time is moving. The faster an object travels, the more slowly time passes for that object, as measured by a stationary observer. Perhaps even more astonishing, **one person's past could theoretically be another's future** – which is why Einstein described the past, present and future as 'persistent illusions.'" [bold in original]

One way in which our understanding of time was affected by Einstein's relativity is often described using a thought experiment called "the twins paradox" wherein a hypothetical set of twins are separated and one is placed on a spaceship that travels near the speed of light; the second twin remains on Earth. The spaceship takes the traveling twin away from Earth for two and a half years then returns taking a total of five years for the journey. When the twins reunite on Earth, the traveling twin is five years older, while the earthbound twin has aged thirty-six years.

The Arrow of Time

Another notable physicist of modern times is Stephen Hawking, whose stated intention is to unify Einstein's general theory of relativity with quantum mechanics. Hawking's accomplishments are legendary in his field of astrophysics, but he attained worldwide acclaim when he wrote *A Brief History of Time*, a book that remained on the New York Times Bestseller List for almost two years. He frequently writes for scientific publications but this book addressed a popular audience rather than an academic one. The title gives away but one focus of this book, for it is at least equally about cosmology, astrophysics, quantum physics and, of course, his ideas about black holes, which is an area of special interest for Hawking.

One of the many topics Hawking discusses in his book is *The Arrow of Time*: "There are at least three different arrows of time. First, there is the thermodynamic arrow of time, the direction of time in which disorder or entropy increases. Then, there is the psychological arrow of time. This is the direction in which we feel time passes, the direction in which we remember the past but not the future. Finally, there is the cosmological arrow of time. This is the direction of time in which the universe is expanding rather than contracting." The thermodynamic arrow of time seems to be mostly a matter of probability; disorder is more broadly defined than order (there may be only one state that is defined as ordered, such as a whole ceramic cup, while there are innumerable ways in which the molecules and atoms that form the cup could be disordered) so the tendency toward disorder seems appropriate. The psychological arrow of time is determined within the brain by the thermodynamic arrow of time. Hawking phrased it thusly, "Disorder, or entropy, increases with time because we measure time in the direction in which disorder increases. You can't have a safer bet than that!"

We see then that the physical, psychological, and cosmological arrows of time all seem to point the same direction, though physical time, as we learned from Einstein, depends on your frame of reference, and in accord with the quote that begins this chapter, psychological time can vary with your frame of mind. Existence moves from order to disorder, we remember the past, the universe continues to expand and time marches on.

Bang!?

Cosmologically we observe that the universe is expanding and that entropy is increasing with the passage of time. Therefore, we calculate that if we could reverse entropy and expansion we would eventually find the entire universe, highly ordered, in an infinitely small space called a singularity. (Realize that "infinite space" is as much an oxymoron as "eternal time" and that a more accurate way to phrase it is to say that a singularity is a marker for where matter and energy has been and continues to be compressed to such high density that it is squeezed or sucked out of spacetime. This would apply in the situation of black holes, which are singularities in spacetime; the particular singularity in this case, which would create spacetime, could not occur *in* spacetime but in an arena that we have yet to comprehend.)

Imagine all space and the contents of space, galaxies, solar systems, all life, and time itself compressed to a point of nothingness like a coiled spring in search of release. Literally out of nowhere (because "where" doesn't exist yet) a tremendous explosion occurs; but if you just made a picture of it in your mind, make sure you picture it from inside the explosion rather than outside, because inside that explosion, what science calls the "Big Bang," is where everything unfolds. Existence is not the result of the Big Bang so much as it is the current state of the Big Bang, and it is the continuing expansion from this explosion that points the cosmological arrow of time.

British physicist Paul Davies picks up on the Big Bang in *The Mind of God*, "The picture that we then obtain for the origin of the universe is a remarkable one. At some finite instant in the past the universe of space, time, and matter is bounded by a space-time singularity. The coming-into-being of the universe is therefore represented not only by the abrupt appearance of matter, but of space and time as well." He continues with, "Where did the big bang occur? The bang did not occur at a point in space at all. Space itself came into existence with the big bang. There is similar difficulty over the question: What happened before the big bang? The answer is, there was no 'before.' Time itself began at the big bang."

This perspective is valid when considering the world we know and watch and live in; in the world of subatomic particles the rules are not so clearly written. The world of quantum physics is a weird world indeed.

The Quantum Leap

While Einstein's work in relativity was a giant step forward in our understanding of the fundamental workings of the universe, quantum physics was another. Both offer viable theoretical explanations of how things work in the world, but they disagree on a few points. Continuing work in the field (i.e., Hawking's stated goal of uniting relativity and quantum physics) is directed at reconciling those differences. An article in Discover Magazine (June 2007) by Tim Folger elaborates on another scientific view of time:

"The problem, in brief, is that time may not exist at the most fundamental level of physical reality. If so, then what is time? And why is it so obviously and tyrannically omnipresent in our own experience? 'The meaning of time has become terribly problematic in contemporary physics,' says Simon Saunders, a philosopher of physics at the University of Oxford. 'The situation is so uncomfortable that by far the best thing to do is declare oneself an agnostic.'

"The trouble with time started a century ago, when Einstein's special and general theories of relativity demolished the idea of time as a universal constant. One consequence is that the past, present, and future are not absolutes. Einstein's theories also opened a rift in physics because the rules of general relativity (which describe gravity and the large-scale structure of the cosmos) seem incompatible with those of quantum physics (which govern the realm of the tiny). Some four decades ago, renowned physicist John Wheeler, then at Princeton, and the late Bryce DeWitt (1923–2004), then at the University of North Carolina, developed an extraordinary equation that provides a possible framework for unifying relativity and quantum mechanics. But the Wheeler-DeWitt equation has always been controversial, in part because it adds yet another, even more baffling twist to our understanding of time.

"'One finds that time just disappears from the Wheeler-DeWitt equation,' says Carlo Rovelli, a physicist at the University of the Mediterranean in Marseille, France. 'It is an issue that many theorists have puzzled about. It may be that the best way to think about quantum reality is to give up the notion of time – that the fundamental description of the universe must be timeless.'

"No one has yet succeeded in using the Wheeler-DeWitt equation to integrate quantum theory with general relativity. Nevertheless, a sizable minority of physicists, Rovelli included, believe that any successful merger of the two great masterpieces of twentieth-century physics will inevitably describe a universe in which, ultimately, there is no time."

Yet the idea of time passing seems to dominate our thoughts and anything so important must be handled properly, which naturally includes accurate measurement. Seth Lloyd, a quantum mechanical engineer at MIT, tells of a trip to the National Institute of Standards and Technology in Boulder, Colorado where they have the atomic clock that sets the standard for all clocks in the US. Lloyd was informed during his visit that the clocks at NIST do not measure time; time is defined to be what these clocks measure. They define the time standards for the world and time is defined by the ticking of their clocks. In the same Discover article, Rovelli agrees with the NIST timekeepers.

"We never really see time," he says. "We see only clocks. If you say this object moves, what you really mean is that this object is here when the hand of your clock is here, and so on. We say we measure time with clocks, but we see only the hands of the clocks, not time itself. And the hands of a clock are a physical variable like any other. So in a sense we cheat because what we really observe are physical variables as a function of other physical variables, but we represent that as if everything is evolving in time.

"What happens with the Wheeler-DeWitt equation is that we have to stop playing this game. Instead of introducing this fictitious variable – time, which itself is not observable – we should just describe how the variables are related to one another. The question is, Is time a fundamental property of reality or just the macroscopic appearance of things? I would say it's only a macroscopic effect. It's something that emerges only for big things."

"By 'big things,' Rovelli means anything that exists much above the mysterious Planck scale. As of now there is no physical theory that completely describes what the universe is like below the Planck scale. One possibility is that if physicists ever manage to unify quantum theory and general relativity, space and time will be described by some modified version of quantum mechanics. In such a theory, space and time would no longer be smooth and continuous. Rather, they would consist of discrete fragments – quanta, in the argot of physics – just as light is composed of individual bundles of energy called photons. These would be the building blocks of space and time. It's not easy to imagine space and time being made of something else. Where would the components of space and time exist, if not in space and time?

"As Rovelli explains it, in quantum mechanics all particles of matter and energy can also be described as waves. And waves have an unusual property: An infinite number of them can exist in the same location. If time and space are one day shown to consist of quanta, the quanta could all exist piled together in a single dimensionless point. 'Space and time in some sense melt in this picture,' says Rovelli. 'There is no space anymore. There are just quanta kind of living on top of one another without being immersed in a space.'

"Rovelli has been working with one of the world's leading mathematicians, Alain Connes of the College of France in Paris, on this notion. Together they have developed a framework to show how the thing we experience as time might emerge from a more fundamental, timeless reality. As Rovelli describes it, 'Time may be an approximate concept that emerges at large scales – a bit like the concept of *surface of the water*, which makes sense macroscopically but which loses a precise sense at the level of the atoms.'

"Realizing that his explanation may only be deepening the mystery of time, Rovelli says that much of the knowledge that we now take for granted was once considered equally perplexing. 'I realize that the picture is not intuitive. But this is what fundamental physics is about: finding new ways of thinking about the world and proposing them and seeing if they work. I think that when Galileo said that the Earth was spinning crazily around, it was utterly incomprehensible in the same manner. Space for Copernicus was not the same as space for Newton, and space for Newton was not the same as space for Einstein. We always learn a little bit more.'

"Rovelli senses another temporal breakthrough just around the corner. 'Einstein's 1905 paper came out and suddenly changed people's thinking about space-time. We're again in the middle of something like that,' he says. When the dust settles, time – whatever it may be – could turn out to be even stranger and more illusory than even Einstein could imagine."

Two Orders of David Bohm

Physicist and philosopher David Bohm (1917–1992) proposed a cosmological order radically different from generally accepted conventions, which he expressed in terms of the implicate order and the explicate order. Bohm's *implicate order* of reality is "enfolded" in such a way that space and time are no longer dominant factors determining relationships between the elements. Instead, a basic interconnectedness of elements is considered, from which our ordinary concepts of space and time and a world of separately existing things, are conceptualized by the mind. The world we experience, in fact, appears in what he called the *explicate*, or "unfolded," *order*. In his book *Unfolding Meaning*, he talks of time, "Now ordinarily we experience through time, and there are many paradoxes in that because we think of past, present and future. But you see, the past is gone, and the future is not yet, and the present, taken as the dividing point between past and future, divides what doesn't exist from what doesn't exist. So that would suggest that there is no present. Another view though is to say that the actual moment of existence – this present – is in some sense beyond time." In Bohm's revolutionary model of reality, existence is often likened to a hologram, wherein any element of reality contains enfolded within itself the totality of the universe.

When Bohm was a professor at Princeton he wrote a text book and sent copies to Niels Bohr (1885–1962), who coauthored the very popular Copenhagen interpretation of quantum physics, and to Albert Einstein. Bohr did not respond, but Einstein was intrigued and arranged a meeting with Bohm, which was the first of several in which they discussed quantum theory. Einstein was quite impressed with Bohm's view on quantum mechanics and confided that he was just as frustrated with the orthodox Copenhagen approach as was Bohm.

And a Krishnamurti on the Side

While most of his career was devoted to theoretical physics, later in life Bohm became quite the philosopher, and the idea of time was a significant piece of his overall view of reality. *The Ending of Time* is a published book of transcripts that were recorded during several extended dialogues that took place between David Bohm and Jiddu Krishnamurti (1895–1986), world-renowned spiritual teacher and philosopher. The discussions begin with an exploration of the question, "Has humanity taken a wrong turn, which has brought about endless division, conflict, and destruction?" From my reading, Bohm makes an occasional minor point, but Krishnamurti dominates throughout the encounter and leads Bohm along a winding trail that ends exactly where Krishnamurti planned for it to end. You may have guessed from the title and the opening question that the answer to the question is "yes" and that time was somehow at the root of things. Perhaps one might deduce another step and venture that *the ending of time* might be the proposed solution to the problem implied in the question. Though I can't recommend it as a great read, the point of this book is not to entertain, but to exercise the mind, to get the reader to think differently about time. Since that is what we are doing as well, let's consider that conversation.

The discussion develops around the idea that our perception of time is what appears to separate us from the eternal. Bohm talks about how, as far back as ancient Greece, mankind has placed great importance on time, "Let's go slowly because you see, if we go back to the scientific, even commonsense point of view, implicitly time is taken as the ground of everything in scientific work. In fact even in ancient Greek mythology Chronos, the god of time, produces his children and swallows them. That is exactly what we said about the ground; everything comes from the ground and dies to the ground. So, in a way, mankind long ago began to take time already as the ground."

They talk about how we define reality as an accumulation of memories built on the past and Krishnamurti recommends being rid of memory. Seemingly taken aback by such a suggestion, Bohm asks for clarification of the word memory as a record of knowledge, and Krishnamurti responds, "The memory of experiences, hurts, attachments, the whole of it. Now can that come to an end? Of course it can. This is the point; it can come to an end when the very perception asks, what is it? What is hurt? What is psychological damage? The perception of it *is* the ending of it. Not carrying it over, which is time. The very ending of it is the ending of time." What I believe Krishnamurti was suggesting here, and what Dr. Hew Len hinted at in the previous chapter, is that we can see the past for what it is; a tool we use to structure our worldview. While we cannot free our existence in duality from the influence of time, we can sever our dependency on time by simply asking, "What is it?"

Of course, coming up with the correct answer to the question "What is it?" is not really the purpose of this exercise; the point is in breaking the hypnotic effect of time by simply allowing the question to be asked.

When you think about it, our whole experience is memory. We live life in what we call the present, but the science of neurophysiology tells us that the brain is never directly aware of the present moment due to sensory lag. Because it takes time (albeit a very small amount) to process our perceptions, we are not mentally aware of a moment or event until it has actually passed. We also know that starlight travels vast distances and that some of the stars that we will see in the sky tonight could very well have burned out before the Earth was formed. Some are so far away that their light takes millions of years to reach us.

A Bold Move

In the linear view of the mind, everything that has ever happened, has led to this moment, which, in turn, leads to an uncertain future, but in a literal sense, everything happens now in this eternity. The arbitrary and artificial divisions that we call time are integral to the structure of human existence as we know it, but time is merely a device we use to organize that existence, and perhaps even more so, to create a sense of control over what we see as the measure and progression of our lives.

It's About Time

Eckhart Tolle's New Age classic, *The Power of Now*, has been translated into 32 languages and has become one of the most influential spiritual books of our time. In another book, *Stillness Speaks*, he summarizes, "The division of life into past, present, and future is man-made and ultimately illusory. Past and future are thought forms, mental abstractions. The past can only be remembered Now. The future, when it comes, is the Now. So the only thing that is real, the only thing there ever is *is* the Now."

Our sense of continuity is a major factor defining our humanity and it is not the intention here to imply that the past and future are without value. Within the context of duality, the past is a record of our experience and knowledge, while the future is defined by our expectations, which are colored by our fears and aspirations. As practical matters they both have great value and influence in the present. This world of dualities in which we live, exists within time, and, as physical processes, so do we. While the past and future are not real in the present, together they form the foundation on which our perceptions of the present are based. We are immersed in the play of duality, however, and we give time so much power that it has taken over to the extent that in a very real way we are slaves to the clock.

Questioning the reality of time is a bold move against a powerful cultural force; do we dare? If indeed, we are seekers of spiritual truth, then we are obliged to question everything and submit it to a higher authority, higher than the church of exoteric religion, higher even than the church of the mind. Bypass these gatekeepers and submit your questions directly to Sophia for she is wisdom and will direct you to the truth; when that truth is realized, there are no more questions and seeking ends. To that end, shaking up our ideas about something so central to our lives as time is one of many ways that we can begin the essential process of deconstructing the ego.

*"I try to find myself in things but never quite make it,
and end up losing myself in them.
That is the fate of the ego."*

Eckhart Tolle

Chapter Eleven

Deconstructing the Ego

The term *deconstruction* could be interpreted to mean *destruction*, but this will not be the case; our point is more of an analysis than an annihilation. What we are really discussing here, the ego, may be seen as a kind of concept processing and integrating program running on a really cool bio-computer. What we will be doing, what we have been doing throughout this book, is to take this thing apart, see what it is made of, and how it works. Unfortunately, we have only one tool with which to accomplish our deconstruction, and that is the ego itself.

If you prefer to look at the ego as a living thing, another way of thinking is required. In that light, one might also call this process the *disillusion* of the ego, wherein the ego is informed, and comes to accept that it exists solely as the result of conditioned patterns of thought, and does not represent the true nature of our being. Until the ego realizes this, it operates under the false assumption that it *is* the consciousness that drives your existence.

Physiological Self

To our senses, we appear to be solid, confined within our skin, and made of certain materials, but closer observation will reveal that this may not be the whole story. We can begin by considering that the

127

individual is not so much a thing as it is a complex array of processes. The skin in which we seem to live is a semi-permeable membrane that is in constant interaction with the environment. We exchange oxygen for carbon dioxide when we breathe, we consume food and drink and expel wastes, we are injured and we bleed, we were born and just as surely, despite our best efforts to the contrary, we will die and decompose; the environment moves through us as we move through our environment.

One way to look at the individual is to consider it analogous to a wave. British ethnologist, Richard Dawkins, in *The God Delusion*, brings up the subject of waves then quotes computer genius Steve Grand on the matter. "A wave *seems* to move horizontally across the open sea, but the molecules of water move vertically. Similarly, sound waves may travel from speaker to listener, but molecules of air don't: that would be a wind, not a sound. Steve Grand points out that you and I are more like waves than permanent 'things'. He invites his reader to think...

"...of an experience from your childhood. Something you remember clearly, something you can see, feel, maybe even smell, as if you were really there. After all, you really were there at the time, weren't you? How else would you remember it? But here is the bombshell: you weren't there. Not a single atom that is in your body today was there when that event took place...Matter flows from place to place and momentarily comes together to be you. Whatever you are, therefore, you are not the stuff of which you are made. If that doesn't make the hair stand up on the back of your neck, read it again until it does, because it is important."

Psychologically

While the body may exist as a complex array of physical processes, beyond this, there is something that gives continuity to life, an identity that the processes seem to maintain. The identity with which we are most familiar is the result of many other processes that begin at birth.

The infant does not recognize a separation between itself and the environment, but response patterns form and character develops as the child learns separateness by taking on layers and layers of ideas and images in processes that are known in psychology as individuation and personality development. The *stage theory* is a popular technique used in psychology to map the progress of such processes. Psychologist Erik Erikson (1902–1994) has given us a popular stage theory of personality development that manifests as a lifelong series of psychological crises and decision points. Of the eight developmental stages in Erikson's theory, five occur in the first twenty years, and three of those happen before the age of five.

Input from the environment combines with genetic predispositions to guide the ongoing development of response patterns, or person-ality/ego, which will be further shaped by the choices that are made during critical periods of development. Response patterns are set and the first three of Erikson's stages complete when choices are made between a life rooted in *trust* or *mistrust*, *autonomy* or *shame*, and *initiative* or *guilt*. It is during these most formative years that the image of the individual gradually emerges as an entity that seems to be driven toward a future composed of desires and fears that are drawn from a past that is made up of thoughts we call memories and beliefs.

By the time the child enters school, the maintenance and continuing construction of this image requires so much attention that the only reality that is recognized is the constructed dualistic reality. The illusion becomes all the more convincing when the child enters the age of reason and responsibility. There will be expectations and restrictions imposed by various agents and agencies ranging from friends and family to God and country. This is the circumstance in which most people live their lives of quiet desperation; pulled by unseen forces that were set in motion during childhood and even before they were born.

Why Deconstruct the Ego?

The purpose of deconstructing the ego is to expose the ego for the fallacy that it is. In the world of consensus reality, we seek spiritual truth as individuals in hopes of moving toward what we perceive to be a more elevated state of consciousness. In the process we may become better human beings, calmer, more sensitive to others, perhaps charit-able. Enlightenment is another matter altogether. The belief in a separate self is the dream from which we are trying to awaken. The individual, the personality, the ego, can't really cross that line, and as long as the ego remains in control of attention, enlightenment will remain a mystery. No doubt, this produces a quandary for the spiritual seeker. Lonny J. Brown takes up this subject in his book, *Enlightenment in Our Time: The Perennial Wisdom in the New Millennium*, "You are not who you think you are, and you have no idea who you really are.

"You identify yourself with your body, your name, your gender, your family and work roles, your religion, your political convictions, your nation. But all of these are costumes created by your unknown Self, so that you might discover another way home through the cosmic maze of creation. You are a sightseer who has lost your way, and then forgotten that you are lost.

"You act as if you know yourself. You use the same self-referent first-person pronoun 'I' that everyone else does, and believe yourself to be an isolated some-one with a separate, solid identity.

"But you are neither your name, nor your social position, nor your job, nor your part within a family, community or nation. You have limited your knowledge of yourself drastically with circumstantial roles, arbitrary allegiances, acquired tastes, fashionable conventions of thought, unquenchable desires, overgrown fears, and numerous opinions about what is important or possible.

"You have been defined by tribal myths, old habits and blind reactions. You have been a happy slave to your appetites, content to live in the fortified crystal palace of your established personality: Yet, however elegant and comfortable and perfectly self-justified, it turns out to be illusory." The true objective of seeking is not to become a better or more spiritual person, but to shed the illusion of separateness and to rediscover the Oneness of existence.

The Future of the Unhappy Little Me

In *Through the Open Door* Eckhart Tolle claims that we form an image of who we are based on our pasts; he refers to this image, what might also be called the ego, as the "little me." The little me lives in a story that is essentially unsatisfactory, but society and the media tell us that although our story may not be happy at this point, there are happy endings and that it is appropriate to expect them. Tolle talks about how we pursue the future in our search for our happy ending. "It may be material success, it may be finding the ideal partner, it may be reaching a state of enlightenment. The future promises fulfillment, that's why everybody is running towards it." We resist the unsatisfactory present by projecting a future where we will find the solutions to life's problems, our happy ending.

This is only half the story, however, and he goes on to say that the little me, "is drawn towards it [the future] as an answer to its story, but it knows at the same time that the future is going to kill it." The little me understands that while the future is filled with promise, it is also potentially dangerous; things could always get worse and eventually, of course, the little me will die. We see then that humans follow two motivations into the future, and we know them as desire and fear. We write our story by drawing on what we call our past, a chain of thoughts that may have little or no relation to actual events in one's experience, but are encoded by the mind as memory. The mind uses these memories to create an image and then projects that image into a future that also exists exclusively in the mind; the present moment, which is the only part that is real, gets lost in the shuffle.

Tolle believes that a deep, unconscious need for unhappiness is inherent to the structure of the little me. He emphasizes, however, that it is necessary to the existence of the little me that this need remain unconscious, so that the causes of unhappiness can be projected onto other, or the environment, or circumstances. We then can play the responsibility game, allowing credit and blame to become important attributes of experience. Tolle points out that even under ideal circumstances the little me wants so badly to be dissatisfied that without someone or something to blame, it will create unhappiness in the form of boredom.

According to Tolle, the reason for this phenomenon is that the little me "cannot afford to be in a state of non-opposition for long. It cannot afford to be in a state of peace for long. It cannot afford to be in a state of joy for long. It cannot afford to be in a state of love for long." These states are the result of embracing *what is*, and the little me exists only as the tension between past and present, positive and negative, and polarities in general. The little me, the ego, is merely a perspective and its appearance as a separate entity is sustained by its relationship to a supposed other, and its opposition to *what is*.

Being a spiritual seeker does not exempt one from this human frailty; the very act of seeking implies that there is belief in a future that is better than the present. Duality allows us to be as happy as we want in our thoughts of the past or the future; this land of memories and imaginings, hopes and fears is what the little me, the ego, the mind, is comfortable with and this is what it calls reality. What then becomes of the present moment in this scenario? The energy that lives as the present gets invested physically, emotionally and mentally into the illusions of past and the future.

Chronic Muscular Strain

In his recorded lecture series, *Out of Your Mind*, Alan Watts talks about the ego as an abstraction, "What we call our ego is something abstract, which is to say that it has the same order and kind of reality as an hour, or an inch, or a pound, or a line of longitude." We, however, treat it as if it were an organism, when in fact it is an image or an idea of our self. In his view, Watts considers the ego a caricature of the individual, as the individual is not a thing in itself but a feature of the universe.

The illusory nature of the ego is difficult for most people to accept because there is a sense in which we feel that there is something more than just this image, that there is some sensitive core at the center holding everything together, and it corresponds to the word "I." "I" has a mind, a body, thoughts, feelings, relationships; surely, this "I" must be something real, perhaps even physical. Watts claimed to have figured out what physically separates our existence from that of the world outside, "It's a chronic, habitual, sense of muscular strain, which we were taught in the whole process of doing spontaneous things to order." From early childhood we are instructed to do things that are supposed to happen naturally; *love your brother, be nice, straighten up and act right, behave, pull yourself together*. As children, unable to understand abstract feelings, we react physically in the same way we might react to instructions such as *go to the store*, *eat your peas*, or *mow the lawn*. Watts noted that as we continue into adulthood, this chronic muscular strain becomes the physical referent for the psychological image that is the ego.

While the ego, and the associated muscular strain, don't really have a role in awakening, in the dualistic physical sense they are quite important. We are all familiar with tension headaches and the ill effects associated with excessive stress. It is easy to imagine how this muscular strain could affect health by restricting the flow of energy, or chi, throughout the body. Chinese folk medicine, including acupuncture, likely grew out of a similar idea.

Self Enquiry

A simple and popular way to deconstruct the ego is self-enquiry, which is approached by asking oneself questions along the lines of, "Who or what am I?" The object of this exercise is not to define our egoic self in greater detail, but to differentiate the qualities acquired through experience and conditioning, which exist in the mind made duality, from our being, which is nondual. The anticipated outcome of self-enquiry is the recognition that being is *not* a function of the judging ego, but that which contains and is aware of the ego, and that it is through this egoic *mortal portal* that the Absolute experiences itself.

Many teachers have employed the technique of self-enquiry to help their students break down the belief that the ego is our real self. While the principle of questioning reality is consistent across techniques, variations in style are numerous. Most teachers using this approach suggest self-enquiry as a means of getting the ego to analyze itself. We live a life based on memory and anticipation, centering on the idea of being separate from what is other. If, through self-enquiry, we can expose the nature of the ego as a mental construct, we may be able to see through it to the non-conceptual reality that is the background in which existence unfolds.

In one of my favorite books about enlightenment, *Spiritual Enlightenment: The Damnedest Thing*, Jed McKenna presents his own version of self enquiry, which he calls Spiritual Autolysis. Autolysis means self-digestion and in the book, he describes the process for one of his students. "The process of Spiritual Autolysis is basically like a Zen koan on steroids. All you really have to do is write the truth." He continues, "Sounds simple, doesn't it? Yes, that's all there is to it. Just write down what you know is true, or what you think is true, and keep writing until you've come up with something that *is* true."

The student states that there are 360 degrees in a circle. "Sure." McKenna responds, "Start with something as seemingly indisputable as that, and then start examining the foundation upon which that statement is built and just keep following it down until you've reached bedrock, something solid, true."

The student asks how this statement could be not true. The dialogue goes like this:

M: "The question presupposes that there's a circle."

S: "There's not a circle?"

M: "Maybe. I don't know. Is there?"

S: "Well, if I draw a circle—"

M: "I? When did you confirm the existence of an I? Draw? Have you already raced past the part where you confirmed that you are a separate physical being in a physical universe with the ability to perceive, to draw? Have you already confirmed time as true? Causality? Duality?"

The effort is directed at getting to the underpinnings of our thinking process, the assumptions about existence that we take for granted and upon which we rely for our interpretation of reality. If you take even the simplest ideas that we assume to be true and drill down on them, you come to very basic questions about the reality of things. This is similar to what we are doing when we examine the polarities and processes that we have discussed in this book.

McKenna goes on to describe Spiritual Autolysis in rather harsh terms, "This isn't about personal awareness or self-exploration. It's not about feelings or insights. It's not about personal or spiritual evolution. This is about what you know for sure, about what you are sure you know is true, about what you *are* that is true. With this process you tear away layer after layer of untruth masquerading as truth. Anytime you go back to read something you wrote, even if it was only yesterday, you should be surprised by how far you've come since then. It's actually a painful and vicious process, somewhat akin to self-mutilation. It creates wounds that will never heal and burns bridges that can never be rebuilt and the only real reason to do it is because you can no longer stand not to."

McKenna recommends getting your thoughts into print, on paper or a computer, so that you can look at them objectively. Things can look quite different when they're spread out for examination from the way they may look when they are all scrambled up inside your head. "Writing it out allows you to act as your own teacher, your own critic, your own opponent. By externalizing your thoughts, you can become your own guru; judging yourself, giving feedback, providing a more objective and elevated perspective."

Spiritual Autolysis is a very aggressive style of self-enquiry, but others, such as that of Ramana Maharshi, one of the most influential Indian sages of the twentieth century, are less forceful. Maharshi did not talk of enlightenment or awakening, but preferred the term *Self-realization*, wherein the upper case S refers to the One Self rather than the egoic self (lower case s). This Self-enquiry is different indeed from most approaches in that the enquiry is focused, not on the ego, but on the Oneness directly. In *Talks with Ramana Maharshi* he speaks of this Self, "So I say, the Self is not reached. You are the Self. You are already That. The fact is that you are ignorant of your blissful state. Ignorance supervenes and draws a veil over the pure Bliss. Attempts are directed only to remove this ignorance. This ignorance consists in wrong knowledge. The wrong knowledge consists in false identification of the Self with the body, the mind, etc. This false identity must go, and what remains only is the Self." When asked by what means this false identity will be removed, Maharshi answered, "By inquiry into the Self."

Though on the surface there appears a clear distinction between enquiring into the self, as ego, and enquiring into the Absolute, they lead to the same destination. The first, and more popular, method of self-enquiry is directed at calling the ego at its own game by making it justify itself in its own terms, which, of course, it cannot do as it is an illusion. The successful execution of this method will result in an ego that is aware of its illusory nature and acknowledges that the One is truly in control. Inquiring into the One Self, on the other hand, is to place one's attention beyond the ego, thereby demonstrating to the ego that it has no substance. In either case, the point is to look past who you think you are to discover what you are, to realize that your being and the Divine Being are One.

Spontaneous Deconstruction

While overt activities, such as meditation and self-enquiry, are designed to reduce the influence of the ego, the deconstruction of the ego can occur spontaneously under some circumstances. The trauma of either emotional or physical loss can so weaken the ego that Oneness can be realized. My life threatening illness was not what one would call a near death experience, but it was sufficiently traumatic that I was able to reset many of my conditioned thought processes.

Three years later, in 2003, we were settling in to a new life in Arizona. I still was in quite a lot of pain, but no longer taking the narcotic pain medications my doctors prescribed. I had also left behind the wheelchair and the walker that for many months were the only way I could get around. I had been writing about seeking truth for only a few months when I walked outside one day in August and watched as all the conditioning that had shaped my existence became transparent and revealed the Oneness.

Another way in which the ego can be spontaneously deconstructed is in the natural process of aging. The first 25 years of life, give or take, is mostly a learning process wherein we develop our personalities and gather the tools, such as education, that we will need to carry out our responsibilities as individuals in the world. For roughly the next 40 years, we are expected to contribute to society through personal effort. This includes not only making an economic contribution, but also fulfilling expectations and roles such as having children and starting them on the path to becoming contributing individuals.

In the later years of life, we are faced with the seemingly inevitable deterioration of the body, which, in turn, will alter the ego, as it is the image of who we think we are. We can deny it, and with modern cosmetic surgery, we can hide it to some extent, but we cannot seem to escape the aging process entirely. The ego can also become fearful or bitter as the process of aging takes its toll.

It is how the ego accepts these changes that determine the outcome. The success or failure of such events to bring about awakening hinges on whether the ego embraces the circumstance as *what is*, or resists the now because the ego is unhappy about the current state of *what is*, and/or is afraid of its impending dissolution. Faced with dissolution, the ego will either concede that it is nothing more than a function of the universe, or it will vigorously rally to defend its individuality.

Parting Shots

Spiritual practices designed to weaken the ego can precede awakening, but if it is not yet ripe, the ego can actually be strengthened by spiritual practice because its image is now more spiritual. The "me" has been improved because of what "I" do; "I" meditate, practice yoga, eat healthy holistic food, "I" follow the teachings of so and so, right up to the claim that "I" am enlightened. As much as the ego likes to define our existence in terms of I am this or I am that, in so doing we identify with duality where the ego believes it is in charge. True spiritual progress begins only when we comprehend that there is nothing that can be done to realize the Oneness apart from accepting that the ego is part of the dream from which we are trying to awaken, and that from the enlightened perspective, the ego and the apparent individual who wants to be enlightened are illusory.

Suppose this deconstruction effort is successful and enlightenment occurs; could the ego be damaged in the process? That depends, to some degree, on from which side of the issue you are making the call. The field of psychology generally considers ego strength a good thing, therefore anything that weakens the ego couldn't be good, right? One might intuitively sense that as the influence of the conditioned mind withdraws, ego strength would fall to near zero. From the view of the ego, it will probably resist the idea of relinquishing control of awareness and this may be stressful. Eventually, the ego understands that it is but an image created in a world made by the mind and accepts enlightenment as its true nature. Once the ego truly stops resisting *what is*, it does not cease to exist, as some teachings claim, but becomes an ego without conflict, and psychologists tell us that an ego that is not in conflict is a healthy ego.

From birth, we are under the influence of the groups to which we belong. These groups define us by nationality, gender, age, education, occupation, political affiliation, socioeconomic status, and more. Being civilized also requires that we accept many assumptions about life, including the various roles that we are expected to play. Living in duality necessitates that we exist as individuals, and I hope that this chapter has conveyed how complex and compelling it is to be an individual. Dualism is the product of the mind and contains our experience of life as an individual. It is an amazing construct full of wonder and worthy of thorough examination and understanding.

The real you, the Self, however, exists simply as the background where all these aspects of the ego and mind play with attention, and try to interpret the patterns in this amazing dance of energy that we experience as life. All that stands between you and the Divine is the ego, and it is just an idea. Now we will leave the illusory individual behind so that for the next two chapters we can focus on Oneness from the perspective of nonduality.

*"Talk as much philosophy as you like,
worship as many gods as you please,
observe ceremonies and sing devotional hymns,
but liberation will never come, even after a hundred aeons,
without realizing the Oneness."*

Adi Sankara

Oneness

"All the Buddhas and all sentient beings are nothing
but the One Mind, beside which nothing exists.
It is like the boundless void,
which cannot be fathomed or measured.
It is that which you see before you."

Huang Po

Chapter Twelve

Unity

Central to the wisdom of Sophia Perennis is the quality of unity. In the minds of most people, unity means a coming together of individuals or things, but Sophia's unity is primary and transcendent, seeing the individual and reality in general, as merely expressions of the Absolute. Unity, in the sense we are talking about in this book, refers to the nondual Oneness of reality, not to a conglomerate of individuals and things.

People who are educated in religion and philosophy will occasionally be touched by the eternal wisdom as they examine the various teachings that have been born of our attempts to explain the inexplicable. Joseph Campbell spent most of his life studying, teaching, and speaking publicly on the subjects of mythology and religion. In a recorded interview with Bill Moyers, Campbell spoke of this unity as "a metaphysical realization that you and the other are one, and that the separateness is only an effect of the temporal form of sensibility of time and space, and our true reality is in that unity with all life. It is a metaphysical truth that becomes spontaneously realized because it's the real truth of your life."

Unity in Psychology

For most of the history of psychology, efforts have been directed toward the analysis and correction of what society has defined as dysfunctional behavior. Unlike many of his contemporaries, psychologist, Abraham Maslow (1908–1970) studied healthy, successful people in order to figure out what it was that made them more functional, happier, and well adjusted than the norm.

Maslow is best known for his *hierarchy of needs*, which describes how people are motivated by various needs, beginning with the most basic *physiological needs* like food and shelter. Only when these needs are adequately addressed, does the principal motivation of the person move to the next level, which is freedom from physical threat, or what Maslow called *safety needs*. When safety needs are satisfied, then one seeks the company of others to address *affiliation* needs, followed by *esteem* needs, and the need for *self-actualization*. The first four motivations are based on deficiency, and fulfill the needs of the individual existing in time. Maslow saw self-actualization, however, as more of an expansion, wherein the needs of the individual become secondary to the unfolding of the One. The individual appears to be in harmony with the environment and all that is other, and rather than being in opposition to the moment, the individual unfolds as part of a basic unity of all existence.

An important factor in Maslow's theory is the "peak experience", which occurs as exceptionally blissful and exhilarating moments in life, bringing sudden feelings of intense joy and well-being, awe, and possibly involving an experience of transcendental unity and awareness of spiritual truth. They usually come on unexpectedly and are often triggered by meditation, powerful feelings of love, great art or music, the beauty of nature, or sometimes through using various natural or synthetic psychotropic substances, such as cannabis, peyote, LSD, or DMT.

Conversely, the peak experience can sometimes be sparked by extremely challenging circumstances such as a severe illness or near death experience. Maslow describes the highest peaks as "feelings of limitless horizons opening up to the vision, the feeling of being simultaneously more powerful and also more helpless than one ever was before, the feeling of great ecstasy and wonder and awe, the loss of placing in time and space." When a peak experience is particularly compelling, the sense of the egoic self dissolves into an awareness of a unity with all that exists.

What Maslow considered the happiest, most well developed, fully human persons, he called *Self-actualized*. Self-actualization results from repeated peak experiences and the ongoing satisfaction of the highest needs defined by his hierarchy. Unlike the more base needs of the individual, which when satisfied are left behind for the pursuit of higher level needs, Self-actualization is its own motivation, and the more this need is satisfied, the more likely one will remain in this state of unity and harmony.

Originally, there were five levels in Maslow's hierarchy, but it was revised by him in 1970 to seven levels, and revised again in the 1990's by his successors. In both Maslow versions self-actualization was the highest need. In the latest version, which is not universally accepted, there are eight levels, with the highest being called "transcendence".

Making reference to "peak experiences," as described by Maslow, transpersonal psychologist Stanislav Grof, in *Psychology of the Future* speaks of unity in this way, "…we have a sense of overcoming the usual fragmentation of the mind and body and feel that we have reached a state of unity and wholeness. We also transcend the ordinary distinction between subject and object and experience an ecstatic union with humanity, nature, the cosmos, and God."

Another transpersonal psychologist, Jenny Wade, devised an unusual stage theory that measures the development of consciousness itself rather than any specific aspect of consciousness, such as personality, intelligence, ego development or moral reasoning. Her fresh approach continues to deviate from most stage theories in that it considers consciousness not only as it relates to a living body, but includes both pre-birth and post-death consciousness. At each of her nine stages, certain characteristics of consciousness are observed and categorized; the last and most highly developed stage she calls Unity Consciousness.

Wade summarized the stages in a concise table format that compares the characteristics typical to each stage across a spectrum of measurements. In the following table the measurement categories are in the left column and the characteristics she attributes to this final stage of human consciousness are on the right:

Primary motivation	None - merely living in the Ground of All Being
Ultimate value	None
Attitude toward life	Non-attachment
Perception of death	There is no death except cessation of the body Everything is immortal and constantly transmuting, therefore there is no attachment to life or death because each contains the other
Self boundaries	None; the self is the same as Cosmic Consciousness Recognition of the body-limited self that exists in historical time, but it and the Absolute Self interpenetrate in this material plane
Temporality	Holonomic - Grounded in the Eternal Now but also existing in historical time
Concept of other	There are no others in the Absolute sense Recognition of the bounded selves that exist in the material plane as multiplicities of the One Nonattached appreciation and compassion for, and identification with, others who are perfect as they are but are also suffering from attachment
Locus of control	Internal as free will expresses the Ground of All Being and emanates from it
Level of abstraction	Holonomic Direct, unmediated apperception of all phenomena Fully integrated Newtonian and non-Newtonian realities
Options for action	Infinite and unbounded by the physical plane, except for eventual physical death
Correct option	Only correct options exist

Only correct options exist because this level of consciousness sees reality from the side of unity rather than the perspective of the individual ego, therefore, there is no vested interest in the outcome of events. When there is only one, it's all good.

The Philosophy of Unity

In the Eastern traditions, religion and philosophy blend harmoniously into one teaching, whereas in the West, they are usually separate and frequently in conflict. In *Mysticism and the New Physics*, Michael Talbot (1953–1992) reminds us of the dramatic model of Alan Watts, as he talks about the cosmology of Hinduism. "There is a Hindu myth about the Self of the universe that perceives all of existence as a form of play. However, since the Self is what there is, and is all that there is, it has no one separate to play with. Thus, according to the Hindu tradition, it plays a cosmic game of hide-and-seek with itself. It assumes a kaleidoscope of faces and façades – a dazzling infinity of masks and forms until it has become the living substance of the entire universe. In this game of hide-and-seek it can experience ten billion lifetimes, see through ten billion eyes, live and die ten billion times. Eventually, however, the Self awakens from its many dreams and remembers its true identity. It is the one and eternal Self of the cosmos."

David Loy, in *Nonduality: A Study in Comparative Philosophy*, talks about how duality and the idea of separation break down when closely examined. "It is due to the superimpositions of dualistic thinking that we experience the world itself dualistically…as a collection of discrete objects (one of them being me) causally interacting in space and time. The negation of dualistic thinking leads to the negation of this way of experiencing the world. This brings us to the second sense of nonduality: that the world itself is nonplural, because all the things 'in' the world are not really distinct from each other but together constitute some integral whole."

Ken Wilber has written about thirty books so far. He has formed a teaching, in fact a university, focusing on what he calls integral studies, which incorporates psychology, philosophy, mysticism, ecology, and spiritual evolution. From the start, he has been both influential and controversial. In 1977, he wrote *No Boundary: Eastern and Western Approaches to Personal Growth*, a book that is very much about unity. Wilber believes that we *are* our experience. From the chapter *No-Boundary Awareness*, Wilber adds this to our discussion, "Now when you understand that there is no gap between 'you' and your experiences, doesn't it start to become obvious that there is no gap between 'you' and the world which is experienced. You do not have a sensation of a bird, you are the sensation of a bird. You do not have an experience of a table, you are the experience of the table. You do not hear the sound of thunder, you are the sound of thunder. The inner sensation called 'you' and the outer sensation called 'the world' are one and the same sensation. The inner subject and the outer object are two names for one feeling, and this is not something you *should* feel, it is the only thing you *can* feel.

"That means that your state of consciousness right now is, whether you realize it or not, unity consciousness. Right now you *already* are the cosmos, you *already* are the totality of your present experience. Your present state is always unity consciousness because the separate self, which seems to be the major obstacle to unity consciousness, is always an illusion. You needn't try to destroy the separate self because it isn't there in the first place. All you really have to do is look for it, and you won't find it. That very not-finding is itself an acknowledgment of unity consciousness. In other words, whenever you look for your 'self' and don't find it, you momentarily fall into your prior and real state of unity consciousness." Wilber is one among the many who believe that enlightenment, the state of unity consciousness, is our natural state, and that the ego and the duality on which it thrives, exist only as a delusion.

The Physics of Unity

This sense of unity is often spoken of in relating mystical experiences and in metaphysical teachings, especially those of an Eastern flavor. Physicist Fritjof Capra, in his landmark book, *The Tao of Physics; An Exploration of the Parallels between Modern Physics and Eastern Mysticism*, examines the teachings of the East and compares them to the theories of modern physics. "The most important characteristic of the Eastern world view – one could almost say the essence of it – is the awareness of the unity and mutual interrelation of all things and events, the experience of all phenomena in the world as manifestations of a basic oneness." In the same chapter he quotes fellow physicist David Bohm. "One is led to a new notion of unbroken wholeness which denies the classical idea of analyzability of the world into separately and independently existing parts... We have reversed the usual classical notion that the independent 'elementary parts' of the world are the fundamental reality, and that the various systems are merely particular contingent forms and arrangements of these parts. Rather, we say that inseparable quantum interconnectedness of the whole universe is the fundamental reality, and that relatively independently behaving parts are merely particular and contingent forms within this whole." Capra continues in his own words to say, "Quantum theory has abolished the notion of fundamentally separate objects, has introduced the concept of the participator to replace that of the observer, and may even find it necessary to include the human consciousness in its description of the world. It has come to see the universe as an interconnected web of physical and mental relations whose parts are only defined through their connections to the whole." Many respected physicists have now come to consider the unity of all existence as being elemental to their science. Capra and others who have dragged this view into the public eye generally have risked their standing in academic circles, but in doing so have fueled the fires under a spectrum of modern spiritual and philosophical lines of thought that began to emerge en masse around the mid 1960's.

Into the New Age

Throughout recorded history there have been those who were not completely satisfied with the spiritual options (or lack thereof) offered by their familiar and cultural environment. During much of the Common Era (CE) and before, most of those who chose to approach the relationship between God and man in novel ways were branded heretics, blasphemers, or witches, and treated accordingly. Before the beginning of the twentieth century, choices were limited by geography and communications. Fortunately, much has changed in these modern times and, at least in the United States, there is access, there is knowledge, there is communication, there is the Internet, and the options for spiritual freedom and education are virtually unlimited.

Alan Watts was on the scene in the early 1960's at the start of the Cultural Revolution when the New Age, among other things, was conceived. Probably the most widely read of the two dozen or so spiritually oriented books he authored was *The Book On the Taboo Against Knowing Who You Are.* Regarding unity, in the final chapter Watts writes this, "Yet we can still awaken the sense that all this, too, is the self – a self, however, which is far beyond the image of the ego, or of the human body as limited by the skin. We then behold the Self wherever we look, and its image is the universe in its light and in its darkness, in its bodies and in its spaces. This is the new image of man, but it is still an image. For there remains – to use dualistic words – 'behind,' 'under,' 'encompassing,' and 'central' to it all the unthinkable IT, polarizing itself in the visible contrasts of waves and troughs, solids and spaces. But the odd thing is that this IT, however inconceivable, is no vapid abstraction: it is very simply and truly yourself."

In *The Myth of Enlightenment: Seeing Through the Illusion of Separation*, German born artist, author, and spiritual teacher, Karl Renz addresses unity in this way. "There's no creator and no creation. There's only the one Self and its unfolding, which is infinite. Because there's nothing outside the Self, there can't be a separate creator or creation. Out of this unfolding, the 'I' as awareness becomes the thought 'I am'; from the thought 'I am' comes the feeling 'I am an object in time.' All this takes place as part of the Self's unfolding."

Some express concern that unity consciousness does not emphasize personal responsibility, as does the dualistic perspective. Lonny Brown addresses this issue in *Enlightenment in Our Time*, where he writes under the subject *Unity Awareness*, "Ultimately, the dichotomy between subject and object is a false one; any sense of separation between you and the entirety of the universe is actually imaginary, albeit functional within the everyday world of time and space. When you realize this, it means that you needn't take your battles too seriously, for everyone you confront is yourself, if in disguise. Furthermore – and this is real blasphemy to the religious establishment – there's no difference between sacred and profane... it all depends on where you're coming from. You are instantly purified by your highest intentions.

"Finally understanding the abiding fundamental fact of unity-in-multiplicity, every experience and contact automatically unites and enlightens. There is no longer any local source of truth, no personal territory to protect, and no enemy to ward off. There is only the ALL.. being.

"Does this mean that saving money, brushing your teeth and opposing crime is unenlightened? Hardly. It means that with increasing realization, our actions come not from desperation and fear, but from wisdom, harmony and humor. We may perform the very same tasks, yet from a much more spacious perspective. We can be at once fierce and free."

In *The Laughing Jesus*, Timothy Freke and Peter Gandy promote a Gnostic perspective of the teachings of Jesus, and they talk of unity in the last chapter of their book. What they speak of as Literalism, we have discussed as Fundamentalism. "The good news is we are all one. The bad news is only a small minority of us realizes this. Most of us are asleep in the nightmare of separateness. And the misguided conviction that we are separate from each other is the cause of untold suffering. It is the root cause of all our individual troubles. And it is the root cause of our present world crisis created by 9/11 and its aftermath. For Gnostics the only solution is to wake up to oneness and reject Literalism. Because Literalism is, above all, the mistake of taking ourselves literally as separate individuals." I must take issue with their use of the word "mistake", however, as it has always been my sense that in a truly unified existence there are no mistakes and no injustices because there is no one to make a mistake, no mistake to be made, and no one to pass judgment.

The New Age has made available to the world a diversity of choices in spiritual paths and nondual teachings that has not been experienced before in our history. There is, however, no path that takes you to enlightenment, or unity, or true peace. In a unified consciousness there is no path because there is no one to walk it, nowhere to go, nothing to become, nothing to fix. The unity that we have described in this chapter is the view of the awakened consciousness, which we will talk about at length in the next chapter.

"Awake.
Be the witness of your thoughts.
You are what observes,
not what you observe."

The Buddha

Chapter Thirteen

Awakening

Like all words "awakening" is a symbol; here presented as squiggly lines on paper that represent a sound, that represents a mental construct, that represents a concept, that is based on a perception of an experience. Like most words, "awakening" will represent a different construct for each context in which it is used. Most commonly, it represents the idea of a return to consciousness after a period of sleeping and/or dreaming, and it is this meaning, which is often used as an analogy for spiritual awakening.

Some Dream Analogies

Analogies are one tool we use to talk about this ineffable subject and awakening from a dream is among the more popular analogies used. When utilizing this method we must keep in mind that analogies merely describe a known situation that is, in some respect, similar to the situation at which the analogy points. An important part of taking this or any other approach that points to spiritual truth is to remember that the map is not the territory, just as the thought of food or water will not nourish your body; do not mistake anything that the mind conceives as being real or true. Attempts to do so are very dangerous, having been known in the past to launch mass movements of organized religion.

151

The simplest form of this particular analogy compares regular everyday consciousness to dreaming while asleep, and the enlightened state to being awake. This use points out that we are dealing with a shift of conscious perspective and not a state of mind. Further, when we awaken from a dream we see the drama of the dream as what it is, a play of the mind.

Another more complex form of the "waking from dreaming" analogy compares the enlightened condition to a lucid dreamer, implying that we do not awaken from the dream so much as we awaken within it, such that the dream continues but we know we are dreaming. After awakening (becoming lucid) the drama of the dream, while it may remain interesting, is not so compelling as to represent one's true existence. One becomes aware of a greater existence that both contains the drama and is untouched by it. The dream characters, the activity of the dream, and the source of the dream all are seen to emanate from the one consciousness of the dreamer.

In *Awakening to the Dream,* Leo Hartong elaborates on this perspective, "You, as a dream character, are a temporary occurrence, while you as the dreamer are beyond space and time. When you wake up to this realization, you will be as unconcerned with your personal story as you are with the character you appeared to be in your dream.

"This is not to say that you will be indifferent and without feelings. When reading a good novel or watching a movie, you are aware of its illusory nature, but nevertheless become engrossed in the characters and unfolding plot. In the same way, as long as you appear as a dreamed character (a physical existence), you will not wake up from the dream, but you might awaken *to* the dream."

Losing Your Head

Another analogy for awakening that I first heard used by Alan Watts, became central to the teachings of Douglas E. Harding (1909–2007) who compared enlightenment to discovering that one has no head. Harding described his own enlightenment experience eloquently in his classic book, *On Having No Head: Zen and the Rediscovery of the Obvious,* "What actually happened was something absurdly simple and unspectacular: just for the moment I stopped thinking. Reason and imagination and all mental chatter died down. For once, words really failed me. I forgot my name, my humanness, my thingness, all that could be called me or mine. Past and future dropped away. It was as if I had been born that instant, brand new, mindless, innocent of all memories. There existed only the Now, that present moment and what was clearly given in it. To look was enough. And what I found was khaki trouserlegs terminating downwards in a pair of brown shoes, khaki sleeves terminating sideways in a pair of pink hands, and a khaki shirtfront terminating upwards in – absolutely nothing whatever! Certainly not in a head.

"It took me no time at all to notice that this nothing, this hole where a head should have been, was no ordinary vacancy, no mere nothing. On the contrary, it was very much occupied. It was a vast emptiness vastly filled, a nothing that found room for everything – room for grass, trees, shadowy distant hills, and far above them snow-peaks like a row of angular clouds riding the blue sky. I had lost a head and gained a world." This is a good analogy for awakening because, in addition to not being able to see one's own head directly, your head supposedly contains your thoughts and self-image, and your head is also where your face, which is the most easily recognized feature of the individual, is found. This analogy is directed at deconstructing the ego by implying that you are not your identity, not the contents of awareness (what you perceive) but awareness itself.

A Techno Artistic Analogy

I would like to share with you one of my favorite analogies for awakening, and one that I think has been tragically underutilized. I am talking about stereograms; these are flat pictures containing a three-dimensional image that is hidden from the normal point of view. As you stare intently at the picture and alter your view in just the right way, you suddenly become aware of a form in a three dimensional image that seems to have been impressed into the flat surface.

Two physiological factors account for the phenomena: 1.) Our eyes do not actually see in three dimensions, but when we look out at the world, because they are in different positions, each eye sees a slightly different 2D image. The brain translates those differences into the perception of depth. We need both eyes to see in 3D. 2.) In the way we normally look at things, the lenses of the eyes focus on the surface and the eyes converge (cross just a bit) so they are both looking at the same point. This normal view focuses on the surface of the stereogram, which appears as a pattern of repeating vertical images. The repeating panels are not exactly the same and the 3D image hides in those slight differences. When you do not converge your eyes on a common point but look through the surface of the stereogram as though staring into infinity while maintaining focus on the surface of the stereogram, the separate images viewed with each eye overlap in the brain to reveal the 3D image.

This analogy of enlightenment resonates strongly with my experience in a number of ways. Seeing the 3D image in a stereogram is analogous to awakening because; a.) it does not require special knowledge or abilities, b.) it is not an altered state of consciousness, c.) it requires that you simply look beyond the surface, d.) a fresh perspective opens up another dimension, e.) the hidden image is there even when you aren't seeing it, and f.) some cannot see the image though everyone (with normal visual functions) is capable of seeing it. In my mind, that is a great analogy, and with that, we will leave behind the technique of using analogies to describe enlightenment.

The Qualities of Enlightenment

In their book, *Mystics, Masters, Saints, and Sages: Stories of Enlightenment*, Robert Ullman and Judyth Reichenberg-Ullman share stories of enlightenment through the experience of spiritual icons both past and present. In the Introduction to their book, they tackle the question "What is Enlightenment?" Each occurrence of enlightenment is unique to the individual with whom it is associated. Influences such as religious and cultural background, personal experiences and temperament will affect how enlightenment is recognized and interpreted by the mind. The interpretation of the mind is all we can convey, for the mind is the instrument of understanding and communication. The authors list six qualities that these stories have in common:

"INTERCONNECTEDNESS AND EGO TRANSCENDENCE. A fundamental shift in consciousness from the individual to the whole appears to typify the enlightenment experience. This shift may be described as the dissolution of the self, a merging of the wave in the ocean, union with the infinite, abdication of the personal sense of doership, or the loss of a separate identity. There remains no identification with the individual ego or isolated, differentiated self. The individual ego, and personality all continue to exist, but the identification with them is eliminated.

"TIMELESSNESS AND SPACIOUSNESS. No thing or concept remains fixed in time and space. Enlightenment sets into play a moment-to-moment existence. In the words of the Buddha, the only thing that is constant is change. There is a realization of the present moment as all there is and a sense of fluidity that pervades all of life.

"ACCEPTANCE. This is a relaxation or surrender, a revelation or insight that all is transpiring according to a plan or randomness that surpasses the individual will. Struggle ends and gives way to acceptance of a reality free of bondage from and attachment to personal desires, thoughts, and feelings.

"BEYOND PLEASURE AND PAIN. Those who have experienced enlightenment describe rapture, ecstasy, love, or simply a contentment that transcends suffering. In the midst of transformation, however, fear, confusion, disorientation, pain, torment, and even madness are not uncommon, sometimes lasting over extended periods of time. This has been described by some, such as Saint John of the Cross, as the 'dark night of the soul.' Disease and pain inevitably arise and many enlightened ones, such as Ramana Maharshi and Ramakrishna, have died of cancer. Suffering exists but the personal identification with it does not.

"CLARITY. The enlightened mind is spontaneous, immediate, and flexible. Thinking is clear and unencumbered by extraneous and limiting thoughts and emotions. Thoughts are purposeful, direct and in the moment, free of extraneous mind chatter.

"SHATTERING OF PRECONCEIVED NOTIONS. Rigidity, expectation, preconceived ideas and personae give way to a vaster reality and even to a profound realization of emptiness, vastness, or nothingness."

Psychology Again

One psychological perspective of the awakened state was described nicely by the stage theory of Jenny Wade that we discussed in the previous chapter, *Unity*, where she lays out specific qualities of the most highly developed state of human consciousness, which she calls "unity consciousness." Another psychological view of enlightenment is offered in the abstract of an article presented at "The International Conference of Knowledge and East-West Transitions" in December 2000, where Nitin Trasi, MD, author of *The Science of Enlightenment*, summarized his view of awakening:

"Enlightenment is a condition completely unknown to modern science. It covers the psychology of the supra-normal or trans-personal, a realm, which has been completely overlooked by modern psychology. Eastern religions define Enlightenment as the loss of 'ego' or the loss of the delusion of the 'me.' The 'ego' of philosophy is different from the ego of psychology. The average person believes in and identifies with a separate ego or 'me' residing in the body. This is a delusion. The delusion consists not in the me itself but in believing the me to be real, to be an entity by itself, and in identifying with it. This belief gives rise to me-based conditioning, which creates a picture of the 'what should be' based on ego-based desires. When such expectations and demands resulting from this conditioning are not satisfied, there is me-based or psychological suffering, which is avoidable. Secondly, with the belief in the 'me,' the rest of the world is automatically seen as the 'other.' This leads to conflict. This is the me-centred or self-centred living of the average man or woman, with its ego-based suffering resulting from non-fulfilment of ego-based desires.

"When a rare person evolves in psychological maturity to the point where he sees through the me-delusion, he is said to be Enlightened. Enlightenment is a change of perspective from the limited viewpoint of a me to a view of life in its totality. Enlightenment completely transforms the entire outlook of the individual, and initiates a process of reversal of the me-based conditioning. This process of deconditioning is the process of Liberation. Enlightenment and Liberation are not magical processes and do not give a person supernatural powers. Nor do they adversely affect a person's ability to live his daily life or pursue his profession. On the contrary, life becomes simpler and work more efficient. The end-point of this process of deconditioning is a state completely free of me-based suffering, a state wherein no one is seen as 'other,' a state of absolute, causeless compassion. This is the state of Final Liberation, called *jivanmukti* or *pari-nirvana*."

Teachers and Teachings

Many teachings focus on the idea of enlightenment, and seekers are drawn to teachers who lay claim to this ultimate spiritual authority. Teachings of an esoteric nature, here meaning those that have enlightenment as the primary objective, do not usually claim to be the only way to spiritual truth, and a seeker encountering a teacher who makes this exclusive claim should be wary. As it applies to awakening there is much to be said about teachers and teachings; more than enough to fill several chapters, but that would not be to the point of this book. Let me summarize my understanding of this situation.

The circumstance of being a seeker implies that there is something being sought, and the mind assumes that this something will come from another person who has "It," therefore, there appears to exist a relationship between teacher and student. Though true spiritual teachers tell us to look within for our truth, looking without is usually easier for us as we feel that we have looked within, and what we saw was lacking. We seek to fill the vacancy with something that we believe we do not already have, therefore we look to another to supply what seems to be missing. The idea that the seeker is somehow different and separate from what is being sought is not true, but the product of conditioning, and this will be fully understood after awakening occurs.

In addition to calming the mind with meditation or some other practice, much of what a true spiritual path teaches will involve describing enlightenment so that the mind will not be completely overwhelmed when it occurs, and will be able to recognize enlightenment, thereby minimizing the psychological impact of discovering that you, as the ego, are just a very complicated idea. Until we realize this, the conditioned ego appears to be the driver of consciousness. Whether you find yourself seeking enlightenment or what many consider more hedonistic or material pleasures, as I have said before, the ego seeks things that will make it better. Better can be defined as physical strength, financial wellbeing, or any number of circumstances including spiritual enlightenment. The ego seeks only that which reinforces its conditioning. The point is that seeking will not enlighten you, *you* cannot be enlightened, because the *you* that *you* think *you* are is just an image.

Most minds are not prepared to make such a leap without feeling the need for guidance and assistance, so a spiritual authority is acknowledged and invested in the image of a teacher. The teacher is only accepted if the ego feels it can gain something from the relationship. In a time when so many enlightened teachers are appearing on the scene, it is somewhat paradoxical that enlightenment cannot be taught. While many paths claim to lead to a state of enlightenment, the best they really can do is to point the student in the right direction and prepare the ego to recognize the shift of consciousness when awakening occurs.

The True Teacher is Within

Many teachings concede that the true teacher, the one who delivers the realization of enlightenment, must be encountered within, because ultimately there is no without. When nonduality is realized, the idea of being an individual is pushed to the background and the Oneness begins to take primary occupancy of one's life. There will likely be a period of liberation or deliverance during which the ego occasionally reacts to various stimuli, but these attachments to old ideas are eventually recognized for what they are and viewed as simply part of the drama of life. From the perspective of nonduality, life is more like a theatrical production in which you play a part, and you no longer think of yourself as an individual living in a world of things and people, but an expression of the play itself, which is the Absolute. How that expression manifests may make no noticeable outward changes in one's life, or it may rebuild it from scratch; all experience is divine and all expression is unique. Some are called to write or teach, others may be moved to creative endeavors in art or music, perhaps in business or even in politics some will serve the shift toward unity. More often than not, however, the personalities will return to continue living ordinary lives, experiencing the divine in the mundane, all the while knowing that there is truly only One, and that each of us, not as egos, but as raw unconditioned awareness, are That. It is only when the ego becomes attached to ideas and outcomes that we create for ourselves what the Buddha called suffering.

Life goes on and events occur that certainly have the potential to upset one's equilibrium in all sorts of ways. After awakening, however, changes begin to take place in the way we interface with our experience. The difference is seen in the recognition that while life, some of which we like and some of which we don't like, is happening all around us, it is not happening to us so much as we are part of what is happening all by itself, to no one.

*"Each little bit counts, we are all part of the same ground-swell.
The most important question we need to ask is how can
I put my own life in greater alignment with that ground-swell?
How can I do my little one-hundred-thousandth worth
to facilitate that shift a bit further?"*

Peter Russell

Conclusion

*"When we shift our awareness or "frequency"
from self-consciousness– where fear, impossibility or feelings of
separation reside – to cosmic consciousness,
which is in total harmony with the universe and
where none of those feelings exist, then anything is possible."*

Maharishi Mahesh Yogi

Chapter Fourteen

The Shift

In this final chapter we will look at a series of perspectives on a subject most minds hold dear – the future. The future is where we look to find fulfillment, so predicting the future has always been a preoccupation of our species. The history of Western culture is peppered with prophets and prognosticators, many of which specifically refer to the significance of current times. There are also prophecies from ancient and indigenous cultures that clearly point to the importance of this exciting period in which we live. We seem to be in a era of accelerated change, as though time is shifting in such a way that more and more is taking place at a faster and faster pace. As we approach a condition where we struggle to maintain control of our world and our lives, we want most desperately to know what the future holds.

Looking into the future will always be speculative, however, and the perspectives presented here are no different in that regard. Various views will be presented and they differ in many ways, but they are consistent in that they all identify the times in which we now live as a crisis point. We will explore several perspectives wherein crisis describes well our current situation, and in each case there is a danger that, one way or another, we could destroy humanity, and possibly the planet itself. On the other hand, there is an opportunity for a shift of consciousness that can take us into a new and very different world. This

163

chapter and the entire book are about something that is happening as you read these words, and it is effecting each and every one of us, whether we like it or not. How this all shakes out is a story that is still being written. It is being written in the unfolding of the ever present now.

The shift we will be talking about in this chapter is at least three-fold. It is actually just one shift, but it looks like more because it takes place at multiple levels and venues. Currently, the most popular shift related subjects of discussion are associated with the year 2012. In another sense, many will claim that there is an evolutionary shift going on within our species. Some think we are entering the end times of Biblical Revelation and the second coming of Jesus, while others believe that our planet is entering an area of the universe that contains a type of energy that will activate unused parts of our DNA, thereby releasing abilities and understanding far beyond what we experience today. Still others believe that friendly extraterrestrials will come and fix all the Earth's problems, or that unfriendly ones will come and wipe us out. Many are convinced that we are headed for an ecological crisis that is the inevitable result of our attempts to separate ourselves from and dominate nature. Another view of the shift, and the one emphasized in this book, is the mass movement of consciousness from the focus on an individual self, to a view of the Self that includes all of reality.

These are different views of one process, so no one aspect is more important than any other, but the reader may resonate more strongly with one particular take on the matter. We will discuss some of these views, but cannot possibly cover all of the material on this vast subject in these few pages. I reemphasize here that one purpose of this book is to introduce some ideas that may shake up your habits of thinking, and not necessarily to explore all of these views in detail.

Inevitably, both the text of the book and the reading list at the end will suffer from omissions; I have read only a small sampling of the extensive material available, and more is coming out every day. I apologize in advance to those authors who should have been mentioned in this book but were not.

164

History

It is difficult to say when this movement really began. Deterministically, it could easily be traced back to the beginning of time, but I find clear signs that the energy of the world surged beginning around the turn of the twentieth century. In the first decades of the twentieth century, major drama unfolded in the physical sciences as new ideas such as relativity and quantum physics, called for a restructuring of the way science understands our world. The twentieth century also brought us advances in manufacturing, transportation, communications, and the information age, including the Internet, which has made the world accessible via your very own personal computer. The social sciences of psychology and sociology matured in the twentieth century, giving us humanistic and transpersonal psychology, as well as the self-improvement movement. Standout advances in the science of medicine might be vaccines, antibiotics, anesthesia, the artificial heart, organ transplants, genetic engineering, and stem cell research.

2012

Widely discussed in New Age circles as an indicator that large-scale changes are taking place at this time is the fact that a major cycle in the ancient Mayan calendar, which is one of the most accurate calendar systems ever devised, ends on the Winter solstice in December of 2012. The Mayan calendar represents a major anthropological contribution to the knowledge base we are building in this book. Much more than a simple way of keeping track of time, the Mayan calendar is actually a complex array of calendars that tracked all sorts of natural cycles including solar year, lunar year, and the planetary year of Venus. Other calendars in the system had divinatory or ritualistic purposes without any known association to observable events. All these different calendars were overlaid and interlocked in many ways, and the various combinations gave rise to further, more extensive cycles.

The ending of the long count of the Mayan calendar is one of the more obvious and widely accepted indicators, but many other factors seem to align with the predicted date of December 21, 2012. A simple search of the Internet will result in hundreds of millions of sites to explore.

Astronomy

Since the time of Galileo, we have come to accept that Earth rotates on an axis, defining what we call a day, and that it revolves around the sun, measuring a year. You may also be aware that the axis around which the Earth rotates tilts at 23½°, which creates the seasonal effect as the Earth orbits the sun. These phenomena can be readily observed because their cycles repeat every year. Beyond what we can easily monitor without sophisticated instruments, there is another cycle wherein the solstices and equinoxes shift gradually so that the weather we now experience as winter would precess backward through the calendar year. This cycle is called the *precession of the equinoxes* and is the result of a wobbling of the Earth's axis. Astronomically, these movements are cycles, so any beginning or end would be an arbitrary designation, but based on planetary and galactic alignments, the Mayans believed that the winter solstice of 2012 marks the end point of this precession cycle and the beginning of a new age. As astronomy evolved in its early days from astrology, this alignment will also be considered in the relationship of astrology to 2012 and this particular shift.

Another astronomical phenomenon we can talk about is solar cycles. Solar cycles take about 11½ years and are marked by variations in solar activity that effect the Earth in many ways. The most powerful solar maximum recorded since they were first discovered about 200 years ago, took place in 1958 when sunspot activity was so intense that the Northern Lights were seen as far south as Mexico.

Since they were discovered, scientists have been trying to figure out the mechanism by which solar cycles take place and how to predict their intensity. In 2006, Mausumi Dikpati, of the National Center for Atmospheric Research, came up with an explanation and a means to predict solar cycles. Like the Earth, the sun spins on an axis, which gives it an equator. Similar to the ocean currents of the Earth, the sun has currents that circulate the magnetic disturbances on the surface away from the equator toward the poles where they are pulled in toward the core. David Hathaway, of the National Space Science & Technology Center, Marshall Space Flight Center, describes the process, "The top of the conveyor belt skims the surface of the sun, sweeping up the magnetic fields of old, dead sunspots. The 'corpses' are dragged down at the poles to a depth of 200,000 km where the sun's magnetic dynamo can amplify them. Once the corpses (magnetic knots) are reincarnated (amplified), they become buoyant and float back to the surface." This is where sunspots come from, they are recycled. This conveyor belt takes between thirty and fifty years to complete one loop.

A new solar cycle, numbered 24, began in 2008 and it seems to be important to the scientific community. In a NASA press release dated January 10, 2008, Hathaway talks about Solar Cycle 24. "'Solar storms can disable satellites that we depend on for weather forecasts and GPS navigation,' Hathaway says. Radio bursts from solar flares can directly interfere with cell phone reception while coronal mass ejections hitting Earth can cause electrical power outages. 'The most famous example is the Quebec outage of 1989, which left some Canadians without power for as much as six days.' "Much of this is still years away. ' Intense solar activity won't begin immediately,' notes Hathaway. 'Solar cycles usually take a few years to build from solar minimum (where we are now [Jan. 08]) to Solar Max, expected in 2011 or 2012.'"

In a different NASA article, Hathaway introduces another consideration related to solar cycles with the idea of magnetic reversals, "'The magnetic poles [of the sun] exchange places at the peak of the sunspot cycle. In fact, it's a good indication that Solar Max is really here.' The Sun's magnetic poles will remain as they are now, with the north magnetic pole pointing through the Sun's southern hemisphere, until the year 2012 when they will reverse again." This will not be a smooth, quick transition and there will be many solar disturbances in the form of huge magnetic storms. The effects of this activity are not confined to the sun and the area immediately surrounding it, the solar wind spreads the swirling masses of magnetic energy out into and beyond the orbits of the planets to define the edge of what scientists call the heliosphere, which is the area of space affected by the solar wind. The article quotes another solar physicist at the Marshall Space Flight Center, Steve Suess, who has this to add, "Changes in the Sun's magnetic field are carried outward through the heliosphere by the solar wind, It takes about a year for disturbances to propagate all the way from the Sun to the outer bounds of the heliosphere."

Hathaway adds that, "the impact of the field reversal on the heliosphere is complicated." Based on geological evidence explained in the article, we do know that, "Earth's magnetic field also flips, but with less regularity. Consecutive reversals are spaced 5 thousand years to 50 million years apart. The last reversal happened 740,000 years ago. Some researchers think our planet is overdue for another one, but nobody knows exactly when the next reversal might occur." Flip is perhaps a deceptive word leading one to believe that one minute north is north and the next minute north is south. NASA describes a process that takes thousands of years, during which time, there may be multiple magnetic poles that move about as a disruptive magnetic field settles into a more or less consistent dipolar configuration.

Currently, the geographic poles (based on the axis around which the Earth rotates) are different from the magnetic poles. Furthermore, science has known for some time that the magnetic poles move. Another NASA article about tracking the magnetic north pole tells us that, "The pole kept going during the twentieth century, north at an average speed of 10 km per year, lately accelerating to 40 km per year," at this rate the north magnetic pole will leave Canada and be in Siberia within a few decades. Elsewhere in the article, it was also noted that the strength of Earth's magnetic field is decreasing.

The Importance of Magnetic Fields

Earth's magnetic field does much more than cause the compass needle to point north. Earlier we discussed the solar wind that sends out highly charged plasma containing radiation that would cause great harm to life forms on the planet. The earth's magnetic field reflects, deflects or absorbs most of the solar wind that comes our way, thereby limiting the amount and types of energy that reach us. Scientists call the magnetic field of our planet the magnetosphere, and it operates in a delicate balance to support life as we know it.

On February 17, 2007 the NASA "Time History of Events and Macroscale Interactions during Substorms" (THEMIS) mission launched an array of five satellites into orbit to observe, among other things, the earth's magnetic field. Only a few months later a noteworthy event occurred. Another article from NASA tells of a rip in the magnetic field that was observed in June of 2007; "The event began with little warning when a gentle gust of solar wind delivered a bundle of magnetic fields from the Sun to Earth. Like an octopus wrapping its tentacles around a big clam, solar magnetic fields draped themselves around the magnetosphere and cracked it open. The cracking was accomplished by means of a process called 'magnetic reconnection.' High above Earth's poles, solar and terrestrial magnetic fields linked up (reconnected) to form conduits for solar wind. Conduits over the Arctic and Antarctic quickly expanded; within minutes they overlapped over Earth's equator to create the biggest magnetic breach ever recorded by Earth-orbiting spacecraft." Scientist Jimmy Raeder, at the University of New Hampshire, who analyzed the data from the event, reported that, "The entire day-side of the magnetosphere was open to the solar wind."

Another NASA article, tells of an upcoming mission that, "will use Earth's magnetosphere as a laboratory to study the microphysics of magnetic reconnection, a fundamental plasma-physical process that converts magnetic energy into heat and the kinetic energy of charged particles." Scientists had come to understand magnetic reconnection in a certain way, but this breach of the magnetosphere was an unexpected anomaly that didn't fit the rules they thought they understood. To further investigate the what, why, and how of this event, in 2014 NASA plans to launch another array of satellites they call the Magnetospheric Multiscale (MMS) mission. In addition to many other related measurements, MMS will monitor Earth's magnetic fields.

Magnetism and Consciousness

Other important research regarding Earth's magnetic field, comes to our attention via Gregg Braden, who left a promising career in computer science to become an expert on ancient cultures and a bestselling author. In his latest book, *Fractal Time; The Secret of 2012 and a New World Age*, he talks about merging science and spirituality, and the relationship between the earth's magnetic field and human consciousness. He talks about how the magnetic fields shape the migratory routes of animals, and how in a similar but much more complex way, humans seem to be influenced by magnetic fields as well. In *Fractal Time* Braden talks about a study revealing that our brains contain millions of microscopic magnetic particles. "These particles connect us, just as they do other animals, to the magnetic field of the earth in a powerful, direct, and intimate way. This connection carries powerful implications. If Earth's magnetic fields are changing in the 2012 time frame, then *we* are affected!"

Satellites designed to monitor environmental factors such as the strength of Earth's magnetic field, have been in geostationary orbit since 1974. On September 11, 2001 surges in Earth's magnetic field were recorded at the same times that the two planes crashed into the towers of the World Trade Center. This strange reading caught the attention of scientists at the Institute of HeartMath, a nonprofit institution formed in 1991 to conduct pioneering research, and to develop heart-based technologies. They believed that the correlation between the satellite readings and the events of 9/11 were more than mere coincidence. Further investigation revealed that similar spikes had been recorded during other events of global focus, such as the death of Princess Diana.

A great deal of electromagnetic energy is given off by the human heart. The brain has long been considered the seat of the mind, of thinking. Traditionally, the heart has been thought of as the organ of emotion, of feeling. We like to believe that the brain is in charge, but the electromagnetic output of the heart is approximately ten times that of the brain. Braden and HeartMath believe that the electromagnetic energy generated by the human heart can influence the magnetic field of the earth, and that if enough people can generate one positive emotion at the same time, then "A change in the way we feel about ourselves and our world has the potential to affect the world itself. If the change is a positive one, then the effect of the emotions that result should be positive as well."

Focusing on the timeliness of the 2012 date, Braden adds this, "It may be no coincidence that it's only now – in the last years of the darkest part of our cyclic journey through the heavens, just when we are faced with the greatest threats to our future and even our survival – that we have discovered we have the ability to cooperate with one another in a way that is unprecedented in the history of the world. It's as if we've pushed ourselves to the very edge of our limits and our beliefs. Now we must apply what we've learned in order to survive what we've created.

"We find ourselves living at this rare moment in time when the motion of the universe is converging in just the right way to give us just the right conditions that lead to a shift in the way we think of our world and ourselves. In the same way that we would check the road signs throughout a cross-country trip to make sure that we're going in the right direction, 2012 is like an end-of-cycle reality check. It allows us to think about where we've been, evaluate the choices and direction of our past, and make any midcourse corrections necessary to complete our cosmic journey successfully. This possibility exists only when everything we need to make such a change appears in a single window of time. The 2012 'zone' of alignment appears to be just such a window."

You Say You Want an Evolution

When we think of evolution most people tend to envision a slow process of genetic change taking place over thousands of generations. This is an intuitive view of the situation that makes sense scientifically, and when Darwin introduced the idea in 1859, it caught on immediately. Today, however, we see things a little differently.

Biology, specifically genetics, is the central issue in the evolutionary process; but in order to see the big picture we look to the science of paleontology. What paleontologists found in the fossil records did not support the idea of a steady progression from one species to the next, but sudden leaps, wherein new species just appear. Based on fossil information, it was determined in the early 1970's that evolution was not the gradual progression science had assumed, but occurred by a process that became known as *punctuated equilibrium*. Punctuated equilibrium was the key factor in this innovative theory of evolutionary biology, which states that species populations show little change over relatively long geological periods, but that when a new species evolves, it tends to do so quickly. This is not to say that evolution does not occur gradually as well. Each species evolves slowly over thousands of years, but new species appear in spurts. We must qualify the term *spurts*, however, to stipulate that we are still considering many generations, each showing only minor changes, as we are talking about time on a geological scale.

When a species becomes as complex and intelligent as we are, we have to consider, not just the evolution of the human as a biological species, but of the cultures that we build around ourselves. The culture contains and directs the bulk of our sense awareness, our knowledge, our beliefs, and defines right and wrong. Culture guides the processes of life, giving value and meaning to our relationships, and our roles within society; in doing all this, culture defines the parameters of our reality.

The development of language and writing each required a change of consciousness. When early hunter/gatherers turned to an agrarian life, they began living in larger groups and implemented division of labor. In order to accommodate this cultural change, changes of consciousness were required. Throughout our development as a species, consciousness has shifted. The industrial revolution required that many learn to work and live in shifts, contributing a small repetitive task to the assembly line of production. Now, in the information age, computers, and other high-tech devices designed for communication and entertainment, play important roles in daily life. There seems no room for doubt that our consciousness has shifted to accommodate technology.

Four Phases of Cultural Evolution

Ervin Laszlo is the author or editor of sixty-nine books translated into as many as nineteen languages, and has over four hundred articles and research papers. He serves as editor of the monthly *World Futures: The Journal of General Evolution* and of its associated *General Evolution Studies* book series.

While I have placed the shift as surging around 1900, Laszlo looks to 1800 as the beginning of a process that will culminate in or around 2012. In his book *The Chaos Point* and in *The Mystery of 2012*, an anthology by various authorities on the subject, Laszlo describes the four phases of the shift.

In Laszlo's view, the process begins with *The Trigger Phase*, which began around 1800 and continued until 1960. Technological innovations in the early years of the Industrial Revolution initiated fundamental changes in the consciousness of Western civilization. In the year 1800, there were still no telegraph lines, railroads, paved roads, or steamboats. By the middle of the nineteenth century, however, the Industrial Revolution was introducing an entire battery of new technologies onto the scene, such as advances in the production of textiles, iron, and cement.

Next comes *The Accumulation Phase*, which began around 1960 and ended in 2004. During this period, what Laszlo calls "Hard technology innovations accumulate and irreversibly transform social and environmental relations. They bring about, at an ever-increasing rate,

- "Higher levels of resource production

- "Faster growth in the population

- "Increasing societal complexity

- "Increasing impact on the natural environment"

Laszlo sees the globalization of industrial technologies leading to, "globalizing the economic and financial sectors while leaving social structures locally diverse and disparate." The worldwide social instability created by this movement raised the level of competition for resources that seem to be in short supply and rapidly diminishing. The effect of exploitation on many local populations was that "it degraded the livability of the urban, as well as the rural, environment."

We are currently in the third of Laszlo's four phases, between 2005 and 2012, in what he calls *The Window of Decision*. He sees in our world, the collapse of established values, worldviews, ethics, and aspirations. We are rapidly approaching a critical point in our evolution as we wait for that subtle, but crucial fluctuation that will decide which direction the development of society will take. As we move into the fourth stage, world tensions will rise as ecological, social, financial, and political systems become increasingly unstable and highly sensitive to minor changes in the environment.

Laszlo considers 2012 *The Chaos Point*. He explains his ideas so well that I leave the rest of this section in his words.

"The processes initiated at the dawn of the nineteenth century and accelerating since the 1960s build inevitably toward a decision-window and then toward a critical threshold of no return: the chaos point. Now a simple rule holds: We cannot stand still, we cannot go back, we must keep moving. There are alternative ways we can move forward. There is a path to breakdown, as well as a path to a new world.

"In remarkable – and *perhaps* not entirely fortuitous agreement with the date predicted by the Mayan civilization – the chaos point is likely to be reached on or around the year 2012. The Mayan calendar indicates that the Age of Jaguar, the thirteenth baktun, or long period of 144,000 days, will come to an end with the fifth and final Sun on December 22, 2012. That date, according to the Mayan system, will mark the 'gateway' to a new epoch of planetary development, with a radically different kind of consciousness.

"The year 2012 is indeed likely to be a gateway to a different world, but whether to a better world or to a disastrous one is yet to be decided. At that point, alternative paths open to us:

> "*a. The Breakdown Path: Devolution to Disaster.* Rigidity and lack of foresight lead to stresses that the established institutions can no longer contain. Conflict and violence assume global proportions, and anarchy follows in their wake. or

> "*b. The Breakthrough Path: Evolution to a New Civilization.* A new way of thinking with more adapted values and more evolved consciousness mobilizes people's will and catalyzes a fresh surge of creativity. People and institutions master the stresses that arose in the wake of the preceding generation's unreflective fascination with technology and untrammeled pursuit of wealth and power. By the year 2025, a new era dawns for humanity.

"The insight we get from this four-phase transformation dynamic is simple and straightforward. In society, fundamental change is triggered by technological innovations that destabilize the established structures and institutions. More adapted structures and institutions await the surfacing of a more adapted mind-set in the bulk of the population. Thus in the transformation of our world, technological innovation is the trigger. The decider, however, is not more technology, but the rise of new thinking – new values, perceptions, and priorities – in a critical mass of the people who make up the bulk of society."

Accelerating Evolution

While at Cambridge University, Peter Russell studied mathematics and theoretical physics. Then, as he became increasingly fascinated by the mysteries of the human mind, he changed to experimental psychology. Pursuing this interest, he traveled to India to study meditation and eastern philosophy, and on his return took up the first research post ever offered in Britain on the psychology of meditation. He also has an advanced degree in computer science, and has worked in areas of 3D graphics that paved the way for virtual reality. His principal interest, at this time, is exploring the spiritual significance of the shift we are currently discussing.

Earlier we talked about how biological and cultural evolution seem to be speeding up. Russell has also observed this and contributes to the anthology, *The Mystery of 2012*, by addressing the question, *Why does evolution accelerate?* "The reason for this acceleration is that each new development is standing on the shoulders, so to speak, of what has come before. A good example is the advent of sexual reproduction some 1.5 billion years ago. Until that time, cells reproduced by splitting into two, with each of the new 'sisters' being exact clones of the original. With sexual reproduction, two cells came together, shared genetic information, and produced offspring containing a combination of their genes. It no longer took many generations for one genetic difference to arise. Differences now occurred in every generation, speeding evolution a thousandfold.

"A more recent example is the transition from the Industrial Age to the Information Age. When it came to manufacturing computers, we did not need to reinvent factories or global distribution systems; that expertise had already been gained. We had simply to apply it to the production of computers. Thus, the Information Revolution established itself much more quickly.

"This pattern is set to continue in the future – each new phase requiring a fraction of the time required in the previous phase. In the future, we might expect the same amount of change we've seen in the last 20 years to take place in years rather than decades.

"It is difficult, therefore, to predict what the world will be like in 10 or 20 years. Two hundred years ago, no one predicted we would have telephones or movies, let alone cell phones or the Internet. Just 20 years ago, very few of us had any notion of the World Wide Web or of how dramatically it would change our lives. Similarly, who knows what new breakthroughs or developments will be transforming our lives 10 years from now?" With this, Russell has brought our attention to a process that will be developed further into the idea of the Technological Singularity.

Technological Singularity

In 1963, at the age of fifteen, Ray Kurzweil wrote his first computer program, which was later used by researchers at IBM. In 1968, while a sophomore at MIT, he started his first business, which he later sold to Harcourt, Brace & World. Since he graduated in 1970, he started several other businesses that he sold to major firms. He is the author or coauthor of half-a-dozen books, and in addition to numerous awards and accolades, he holds fifteen honorary doctorate degrees from major universities. Kurzweil has been successful as a businessman, inventor, author, futurist, and recently a movie producer.

One of his many websites is devoted to a movie based on his book, which shares the title *The Singularity is Near*, and is scheduled for release late in 2009. On that website, in an article called *The Amazing Future*, Kurzweil talks about the changes he foresees in the near future. "Within a quarter century, nonbiological intelligence will match the range and subtlety of human intelligence. It will then soar past it because of the continuing acceleration of information-based technologies, as well as the ability of machines to instantly share their knowledge. Intelligent nanorobots will be deeply integrated in our bodies, our brains, and our environment, overcoming pollution and poverty, providing vastly extended longevity, full-immersion virtual reality incorporating all of the senses (like *The Matrix*), 'experience beaming' (like *Being John Malkovich*), and vastly enhanced human intelligence. The result will be an intimate merger between the technology-creating species and the technological evolutionary process it spawned."

This is just the prelude to the real singularity, however, Kurzweil continues, "Nonbiological intelligence will have access to its own design and will be able to improve itself in an increasingly rapid redesign cycle. We'll get to a point where technical progress will be so fast that unenhanced human intelligence will be unable to follow it. That will mark the Singularity."

Kurzweil does not consider the year 2012 to be significant and marks the time of the singularity in 2045, stating that, "The nonbiological intelligence created in that year will be one billion times more powerful than all human intelligence today."

Though Kurzweil concentrates on the technological aspects of our culture, he acknowledges the breadth of this movement into other areas as well. When asked how God fits into his picture of our future, he responded with the following, "Although the different religious traditions have somewhat different conceptions of God, the common thread is that God represents unlimited – infinite – levels of intelligence, knowledge, creativity, beauty, and love. As systems evolve – through biology and technology – we find that they become more complex, more intelligent and more knowledgeable. They become more intricate and more beautiful, more capable of higher emotions such as love. So they grow exponentially in intelligence, knowledge, creativity, beauty, and love, all of the qualities people ascribe to God without limit. Although evolution does not reach a literally infinite level of these attributes, it does accelerate towards ever greater levels, so we can view evolution as a spiritual process, moving ever closer to this ideal. The Singularity will represent an explosion of these higher values of complexity." Another sort of singularity was observed in a very different way by two brothers back in the early 1970s.

McKenna & the I Ching

In their book, *The Invisible Landscape: Mind, Hallucinations and the I Ching*, Terrence McKenna (1946–2000), and his brother Dennis (born 1950), gather perspectives from seemingly diverse areas and carefully build the case for their premise. Their presentation draws one in, unfolding like a mystery novel, but I must advise that this book is not a particularly "easy read," so if you decide to read it, keep reference materials handy and distractions to a minimum, as their style is verbose and detailed. The book is written in two distinct parts.

In Part I, they begin with an examination of tribal culture, they discuss the nature of the shaman, and the use of hallucinogens in shamanistic rituals, wherein the participants attain what is considered a higher state of consciousness. The subjects change quickly as they relate the similarities between the shaman and the schizophrenic. Next, they suggest that science take a process approach to reality rather than a strictly materialistic one, an idea that they buttress by quoting the philosophies of Hans Jonas (1903–1993) and Alfred North Whitehead (1861–1947).

Detailed descriptions and speculations concerning the chemical reactions responsible for perception, thought and memory, both "normal" and hallucinogenic, are presented. Now the stage is set for the experiment, which takes us to the central issue of Part I. The experiment occurs in a tribal setting in the Amazon basin, and consists of their participation in a shamanistic ritual using a natural hallucinogen. Part I ends with an extensive psychological analysis of the experience and the aftermath.

Part II becomes particularly relevant to this chapter as it presents an approach to the Chinese "Book of Changes" or *I Ching*, not as the familiar tool for predicting one's future, but as a calendar of cosmic proportions. The I Ching uses hexagrams, which are sets of six horizontal lines, either broken (- -), representing the yin, or feminine principle, or solid (—), representing the yang or masculine. There are 64 possible combinations of six broken or solid lines, and they are usually seen in an ordered matrix or sequence. Using the standard King Wen sequence for displaying the 64 hexagrams of the I Ching, the McKennas assigned mathematical values to each line and position, then graphed those values at various levels and superimposed these graphs to produce a harmonic fractal wave pattern that they believe represents the "wave function" of reality as we know it. They called it "Timewave Zero."

Timewave Zero is usually represented graphically as a fractal waveform above and approaching a horizontal axis representing time. Various interactive versions of Timewave Zero are available on the Internet. The Timewave fractal ends and touches the axis on December 21, 2012. The concept presented by the McKennas maps a time line that indicates when the greatest likelihood of change, or, more specifically, "novelty," occurs. They consider novelty a movement of consciousness or events in the direction of unity or connectedness as described in quantum physics. The McKenna's theory points out that in our world, where entropy defines the thermodynamic arrow of time, there is a predictable cycle of extropy. In this theory, novelty also represents opportunities for spiritual growth on a universal scale.

Any means of prediction can only be tested as it relates to history, and the McKenna Timewave formula seems to work when traced backward in time. However, it does not predict specific events or locations, and correlates with history to reveal global trends rather than particular localized incidents. In their book, the McKennas point out "that one trend toward greater novelty reached its culmination around 2700 B.C., precisely at the height of the Old Kingdom pyramid-building phase; then a countermovement toward predictable forms of behavior asserted itself and increased in importance until around 900 B.C. At that time, around the time of the consolidation of Mycenaean sea power, the tendency toward habituation was overcome and replaced by a long cascade into greater and greater novelty that reaches its culmination early in the twenty-first century."

They had this to say about the significance of the chosen date of December 21, 2012, "The end date is the point of maximized novelty in the wave and is the only point in the entire wave that has a quantified value of zero. We arrived at this particular end date without knowledge of the Mayan Calendar, and it was only after we noticed that the historical data seemed to fit best with the wave if this end date was chosen that we were informed that the end date that we had deduced was in fact the end of the Mayan Calendar."

Astrology

One might assume that because I came of age in the counterculture of the 60's, that astrology would be second nature to me. I tried, but as it turned out, my logic and reason filter was unable to integrate astrology with my scientific perception of astronomy. Shamelessly, I confessed my lack of understanding of astrology and sought the counsel of Daniel Giamario from nearby Tucson, who has been a professional astrologer for 39 years and represents a branch known as shamanic astrology. I asked him about what is going on at this time and the astrological take on 2012. In an e-mail from Giamario, he writes, "Originally, astronomy and astrology were one. The aspect of astrology relevant to the discussion is that of calendars and sacred time. Ancient astrology and shamanically oriented astrology were inspired directly from the experience of the night sky and the regularity of the cycles and seasons."

"The longest cycle perceivable to the senses, from one lifetime or a number of generations to the next, is the cycle called variously as the 'Precession of the Equinoxes', the 'Great Year', 'the Platonic Year', or the 'Turning of the Ages'. Although different sources cite slightly different exact numbers of years, all round easily into the now well-known number, 26,000." You may remember from our earlier discussion of astronomy that this cycle relates to the wobble of the Earth's axis as it circles the sun.

Giamario explains the astrological ages as he continues, "A result of this 'precession' is to have different constellations of the zodiac appear in a constantly shifting seasonal framework. For example, the stars of Aquarius are beginning to rise with the spring equinox Sun, while 6500 years ago (one quarter turn of the wheel) the stars of Taurus, the Bull, rose with the equinox Sun. Additionally, the dawning of a new age was generally thought of as happening about every 2100 years (twelve months of the Great Year)."

As we are talking about a cycle, determining the beginning or end of it could easily be an arbitrary decision. Giamario told me that in the late 1980's he and a colleague were the first to publish about how to determine the end and the beginning of the 26,000 year cycle. Since then, many researchers, particularly John Major Jenkins, have speculated on the significance of the galactic alignment. Giamario explains how astrology determines the break in this cycle using *the cosmic cross*.

"In the night sky, there are two 'cosmic crosses', the two places where the plane of our galaxy, the Milky Way, intersects the plane of the solar system, seen as the zodiacal constellations. The one between the constellations of Sagittarius and Scorpius is galactic center; and the other one is between Taurus and Gemini, at the galactic edge (anti-center). Over the course of 26,000 years, the Sun at the solstices or equinoxes will align with these celestial crosses. Currently, (and for the only time in 26,000 years), the Sun at winter solstice is on the galactic center cross and at summer solstice the Sun is on the galactic edge cross. Thirteen thousand years ago, it was the reverse. Sixty-five hundred years ago, the spring equinox Sun was on the galactic edge cross.

"The esoteric and spiritual meaning of the winter (December) solstice is of death, rebirth and renewal (the return of the Son/Sun). The Mayans, by placing the end date of their 'long count' at the December solstice of 2012 apparently concur. Shamanic Astrology and sacred astronomy can clearly see in the sky that something 'big' is indeed happening. While there are many opinions about an 'exact date' for the Great Turning, there is no doubt we are circa 2009 right in the middle of the zone."

St. Germain

When my wife, who was raised Catholic, first mentioned St. Germain to me, I thought she was talking about one of the many who have been canonized as saints by the Catholic Church. I soon learned that this person was no ordinary saint, nor is he recognized by the Church, and apparently was (or is, I guess) immortal. Accounts vary, but it is said that he is an Ascended Master who has appeared as numerous famous persons throughout history and was responsible for many great human accomplishments.

In the early 1930's, while living in Washington state, Guy W. Ballard wrote a book about a series of meetings with the Ascended Master St. Germain. The book, *Unveiled Mysteries*, was written under the nom de plume, Godfré Ray King, and it told a tall tale of spiritual adventure. He was shown visions of history long past, and taken to secret meetings of the Ascended Masters. The book was presented as a series of fantastic adventures punctuated by spiritual lessons. In the last chapter of *Unveiled Mysteries*, King and St. Germain entertain visitors from the planet Venus. I will not try to tell the story of the event, but in this chapter, there is much talk about a shift, and the great changes that will be taking place in about seventy years (that was in 1934). The first mention of the shift comes at the beginning of an audio/visual presentation given by the Venusian delegation. "Many changes were shown to take place in the next seventy years. These affected Europe, Asia, India, North and South America, and revealed to us that regardless of all appearances at the present time the sinister force attempting to create chaos and destruction throughout the world will be completely destroyed." They talk about previous periods of cleansing the spirit of both humanity and of Earth. "We are approaching another such period, and this time the release of the Great Cosmic Love, Wisdom and

Energy, the Mighty Rays of Light will not only quicken the minds of the race but the atomic structure of Earth as well making it more 'Luminous' in our solar system. Never, since these Great Lords of the Flame came to earth, have conditions permitted such a Great Outpouring to take place as will occur ere long. Many who have seemed to become hardened by their former activities, will awaken, as it were almost over night, and feel the Nearness of the Great God 'Presence' within each heart. Many, who have been meek and humble but holding close to the 'Inner Presence,' will suddenly blaze forth amazing themselves as well as others by the Transcendent Light they will manifest. All will be done by the Power of God-Love, and humanity will truly begin to realize that it is the height of folly for one part of God's Creation to war against another part.

"There are many throughout the earth who are rapidly awakening, and feeling the Mighty Surge of this 'Inner Light' pouring itself out through them and thus finding greater expression."

Ballard was inspired to teach others what St. Germain had taught him. *Unveiled Mysteries*, published in 1934, was the first of a six-volume set about the "I AM". Along with his wife Edna, Ballard became co-founder of the "I AM" religious activity and "The St. Germain Foundation." He died five years later in 1939 at the age of 61.

Another Alien Connection

Predictions and traditions abound that testify to the significance of this time in which we live. Zecharia Sitchin has dedicated his life to the belief that the Bible is misunderstood history, which, when combined with Sumerian cuneiform texts, points to a very untraditional story of how humans came into existence. Sitchin interprets from these and other documents the existence of a planet in our solar system that has a highly eccentric orbit around the sun. The orbit is like that of a comet, which comes close to the sun, then loops around it and journeys off into deep space only to return again. In the case of this *planet X*, AKA *Nibiru*, that orbit would take about 3600 years. Sitchin's theory holds that an advanced species called the Anunnaki, who inhabit the planet Nibiru, came to Earth 450,000 years ago and created *Homo sapiens* by genetic engineering, combining their own DNA with that of *Homo erectus.* These humans were used as slaves mining minerals that the Anunnaki had come to Earth to procure.

According to Sitchin, the Anunnaki were the gods of old, and we are literally the earthly offspring of those gods. Sitchin's theories have not withstood the scrutiny of serious scientific investigation, but have attracted much attention in New Age circles. Sitchin himself was never associated with the year 2012, but some groups that have formed around Sitchin's teachings believe that Nibiru will return to this area of the solar system around 2012. One concern within this perspective is whether the Anunnaki will be pleased with what humans have become, or will decide that the experiment is a failure and terminate the species.

Hurtling Toward Nothingness

Karen Armstrong has her own view on the shift, and summarizes her perspective on the changing face of Western monotheism in the *Afterword* to *The Battle for God.* "We cannot be religious in the same way as our ancestors in the premodern conservative world, when the myths and rituals of faith helped people to accept limitations that were essential to agrarian civilization. We are now oriented to the future, and those of us who have been shaped by the rationalism of the modern world cannot easily understand the old forms of spirituality. We are not unlike Newton, one of the first people in the Western world to be wholly imbued by the scientific spirit, who found it impossible to understand mythology. However hard we try to embrace conventional religion, we have a natural tendency to see truth as factual, historical, and empirical. Many have become convinced that if faith is to be taken seriously, its myths must be shown to be historical and capable of working practically with all the efficiency that modernity expects." Today, many are taking up the banner of scientific rationalism, because mythos has failed to adequately define the world. Armstrong also talks about how an increasing number of people are rejecting the mythos of traditional religion.

While we cannot expect mythos to take a valid place in our sciences and politics, at the same time we cannot expect rational logos to answer questions about the meaning of life. Armstrong concludes with, "Hence, there is a void at the heart of modern culture, which Western people experienced at an early stage of their scientific revolution. Pascal recoiled in dread from the emptiness of the cosmos; Descartes saw the human being as the sole living denizen of an inert universe; Hobbes imagined God retreating from the world, and Nietzsche declared that God was dead: humanity had lost its orientation and was hurtling toward an infinite nothingness. But others have felt emancipated by the loss of faith, and liberated from the restrictions it had always imposed." I believe there are many others, in rather small but growing numbers, who are coming to realize that it is this same infinite nothingness that is the background, which is the Source of existence.

Prophecy & Revelation

Not all of the changes that have taken place in the twentieth century would necessarily be considered improvements. Even the advances in technology and medicine that have made our lives easier and longer, have also allowed for population growth that may exceed the ability of our planet to support. Science has enhanced our lives in many ways, but the first manifestation of nuclear energy was the most powerful weapon humanity has ever known. Increased interest in spirituality has spawned a rise in fundamentalism that could bring a third world war, which, combined with nuclear weapons, could easily be another extinction event for the planet.

Clearly, we live in the midst of a crisis, and it was not just the Mayan people who saw this historical period coming. Many other prophetic references to current times come from indigenous cultures around the world, and the following are listed on the web site of the Church of Critical Thinking.

- Hopi lore predicts a 25 yr period of purification followed by the end of the Fourth World and beginning of the Fifth.

- Mayans call it the 'end days' or the end of time as we know it.

- Maoris culture of New Zealand says that as the veils dissolve there will be a merging of the physical & spiritual worlds.

- Zulu believe the whole world will be turned upside down.

- Hindus predict the coming of Kalki & critical mass of Enlightened Ones.

- Incas call it the 'Age of Meeting Ourselves Again'.

- Aztec call this the Time of the Sixth Sun. A time of transformation. Creation of new race.

- Dogon tradition says that the spaceship of the visitors, the Nommo, will return in the form of a blue star.

- Pueblos acknowledge the emergence into the Fifth World

- The ancient Cherokee calendar ends exactly at 2012 as does the Mayan calendar.

- The teachings of the Tibetan Kalachakra contains prophesies left by Buddha predicting Coming of the Golden Age.

- An Egyptian calendar in the Great Pyramid indicates the present time cycle ends in year 2012

This has become a topic of such interest that the History Channel designated the first week of 2009 as Armageddon Week and post primetime hours were devoted to a gathering of documentaries about 2012 and the end times. One program in particular, focused on the view of the three Abrahamic religions regarding what is commonly called the End of Days. In each of these religions the end of time is portrayed as a battle between the mythological representatives of good and evil – *God vs. Satan*.

The narrative of the presentation is by Avery Brooks whose booming voice tells us that, "The enduring idea of an apocalyptic ending emerges from the ancient texts in vivid descriptions and hidden clues, revealed and interpreted over time." Based on the information provided in these holy books, we have come to associate the term apocalypse with the idea of destruction and the End of Days, but the word, translated from the original Greek, means a lifting of the veil, a revelation. It is the scriptural accounts and moreover, the interpretations of these revelations that paint such a gruesome picture of the future.

God vs. Satan, which is available on DVD, refers to an early Jewish writing called The Apocalypse of Ezra, which brings the idea forward that "God works his will in history, and that history has a beginning, a middle, and an end, and that the end is something catastrophic." This Jewish idea initiated a belief that would be adopted and modified by both Christianity and Islam. Though embellished in each case, in principle, the idea of a battle between the all powerful

God and the forces of evil remained intact. In Christianity the primary apocalyptic writings are in the book of *Revelation* which ends *The New Testament*. This book was a controversial inclusion into the canon, and has been interpreted to describe the violent destruction of the old world and the beginning of the new. Many Christians believe that the righteous will be spared the worst of the devastation as they are removed from the doomed planet in an action called the *rapture*.

The Muslims tell a similar tale of the future. David Cook, professor of religion at Rice University, is an expert on Islamic apocalyptic beliefs and was interviewed by Deborah Caldwell of BeliefNet.com. When she asked him to summarize what Muslims believe about the apocalypse, Cook said that the beliefs are of two types of signs; *the lesser signs of the hour*, which are likely to happen before the end of the world, and *the greater signs of the hour* that must happen. The lesser signs will be moral, political, ethical, and natural upheavals; most current authorities believe these signs have been fulfilled. The greater signs include, "the appearance of the Mahdi, the messianic figure who brings justice to the world and completes the spread of Islam. Then we've got the appearance of the antichrist who in Arabic is called the Dajjal [المسيح الدَّجَّال]." Many feel that the Dajjal is among us but opinions vary as to whether Dajjal is a person, culture, nation, or ideology. Cook continues, "Then we have Jesus coming down to kill the antichrist. The Qur'an says God will lift up Jesus and return him back, which is usually interpreted as the Second Coming." Cook then explains how the role of Jesus is somewhat different in the Islamic version, "... according to Muslims, Jesus didn't actually die, so there's no issue of Resurrection. As a result, this is viewed more as a completion of his lifespan. In Muslim apocalyptic literature, he lives out a normal life." Once the powers of evil have been defeated, "Basically the world ends. There's no complete narrative, no Book of Revelation to give the narrative unity. But the idea is that God allows the world to end." The Muslim faithful then "go to the highest levels of heaven because they've been purified. Only the best of the best make it through all these temptations. So they stand with the martyrs and prophets. Other Muslims will be consigned to hell or have to spend a little time with their toes in the fire and come crawling into heaven charred."

The Shift

The official position of the major religions regarding the end times is that the scriptures specifically say that no one knows when the final judgment will come. Based on various scriptural accounts, especially in *Revelation*, many, however, especially in the fundamentalist camps, appear to look forward to the end times and find delight in predicting a bleak immediate future for humanity. Perhaps they are confident that they will be saved, they may be anticipating the end of life's struggles, and maybe they just want to be right so badly that, with the promise of heaven for the righteous, they are willing to kill and die for their beliefs. Part of this Biblical prophecy (Rev. 21-1) calls for a new heaven and a new Earth.

A New Earth

What better for a New Age than *A New Earth*, the latest book from Eckhart Tolle. Tolle explains the title of his book, "The inspiration for the title of this book came from a Bible prophesy that seems more applicable now than at any time in human history. It occurs both in the Old and the New Testament and speaks of the collapse of the existing world order and the arising of a New Heaven and a New Earth. We need to understand here that Heaven is not a location but refers to the inner realm of consciousness. This is the esoteric meaning of the word and this is also its meaning in the teachings of Jesus. Earth, on the other hand, is the outer manifestation in form, which is always a reflection of the inner. Collective human consciousness and life on all planets are intrinsically connected. A new heaven is the emergence of a transformed state of human consciousness; and a new Earth is its reflection in the physical realm.

"Since human life and human consciousness are intrinsically one with the life of the planet, as the old consciousness dissolves, there are bound to be synchronistic, geographic, and climatic upheavals in many parts of the planet, some of which we are already witnessing now." In this runaway bestseller, Tolle focuses on preparing his readers to participate in the shift about which we have been talking in this chapter.

Tolle, like many other modern-day teachers, sees this shift as evolutionary. "A significant portion of the Earth's population will soon recognize, if they haven't already done so, that humanity is now faced with a stark choice, evolve or die. A still relatively small but rapidly growing percentage of humanity is already experiencing within themselves the breakup of the old egoic mind-patterns and the emergence of a new dimension of consciousness.

"What is arising now is not a new belief system, a new religion, spiritual ideology, or mythology. We are coming to the end, not only of mythologies, but also of ideologies and belief systems. The change goes deeper than the content of your mind, deeper than your thoughts. In fact, at the heart of the new consciousness lies the transcendence of thought, the newfound ability of rising above thought, of realizing a dimension within yourself that is infinitely more vast than thought. You then no longer derive your identity, your sense of who you are, from the incessant stream of thinking that in the old consciousness you take to be yourself." If this *stream of consciousness* is not who I am, you may ask, then who am I? Beyond the contents and functions of the mind, emotions, or senses, the person who inhabits this New Earth will simply be "the space in which the thought or the emotion or the sense perception happens."

Eckhart Tolle introduced the idea of nonduality to a whole new range of readers with *The Power of Now*; and *A New Earth*, has attracted even more attention. Thanks largely to the enthusiastic endorsement of Oprah Winfrey, these two books have exposed a very wide audience to nonduality. In fact, Oprah created an unprecedented ten-week special web event, in which each chapter of *A New Earth* was discussed in-depth with a worldwide online audience. At the close of the final web cast, Oprah had this to say, "With this magnificent piece of work that you've given to us through your words...as I have read it over and over again, now on my fourth reading, I marvel at how you were able to put these sentences together in such a way that they connect – have connected to me and to all of you all around the world. So thank you for this experience." Presenting unconventional ideas to large audiences, however, invites controversy. Many readers are not ready to deal with the ideas offered in Tolle's books, and his references to Jesus and to scripture have aroused the ire of the loyal Christian contingent.

Christian Ire

I found a well-written article by Russ Wise, titled *The Deception of Eckhart Tolle* at the web site of the Christian Information Ministries. It is emphasized throughout the article that Tolle's teaching is related to the New Age and not to Christianity. It was an expressed concern that when Tolle is quoting Christian scripture, readers might think that his teaching is somehow in harmony with Christian teachings. The author adamantly denies that Christianity has any connection to or approval of the teachings of Eckhart Tolle. One of his criticisms being that Tolle has used scripture and the name of Jesus to validate his own ideas by quoting out of context, but it seems to me that a similar technique was used by St. Augustine to extract the doctrine of original sin from the Garden of Eden story.

At numerous points in the article, Wise refers to Tolle's use of words beginning with upper case, such as Presence, Beingness, Consciousness, Awareness, Spirit, and Source, as implying *deity*. Deity is a term that is defined as the idea of a personal god, but in the eternal wisdom god is not really a personal consideration. To Sophia Perennis, the Absolute is not a Supreme Being; the Absolute is Being Itself.

Another objection talked about in the article by Wise was the similarities between the teachings of Eckhart Tolle and those of Meister Eckhart, the fourteenth century Christian mystic who we introduced earlier. "If one reads Meister Eckhart it does not take long to see the impact he had on his young spiritual adept. Tolle has literally reconstituted Eckhart's teachings from the fourteenth century and adapted them for a modern audience by utilizing current psychological concepts to engage his reader and to couch his argument in a more academic setting. Otherwise, his teachings would be more easily seen as the occultic/New Age ideas that they are and he would not have the potential audience he enjoys.

"Eckhart's thought regarding spiritual 'truths' can readily be seen in Tolle's writing. His previous book, *The Power of Now,* and his current title *A New Earth* are largely rewrites of Meister Eckhart's teachings. Eckhart speaks of the awakening within man to his oneness with the Divine – I Am presence." I personally fail to see how being compared to such a spiritual giant as Meister Eckhart is much of a criticism.

In making this comparison, Wise also points out that the essence of Tolle's teaching is the eternal wisdom, which has come through Meister Eckhart and many others. He reconfirms again the presence of Sophia Perennis in Tolle's teaching when he writes, "Eckhart Tolle speaks of the dawning of a *New Earth* in which mankind will live in harmony – a virtual spiritual utopia – where each individual will fully sense their interconnectedness, indeed their Oneness. This concept, although not a new one to Tolle, has been written about and taught in the occult/New Age realm for millennia." Wise frequently throws in the negatively charged terms "occult and New Age" to devalue Tolle's teaching as illegitimate because it is not Christian or even widely practiced in the mainstream of religious people. This is the way of the esoteric paths, and until the teachings of Christianity were canonized to the cultural standards of the late Roman Empire, the scattered Christian groups we discussed in chapter 4, *Mythos vs. Logos*, could easily be called cults by modern definitions. United and powerful, today, the descendents of these spiritual rebels of history, hold a grim view of the future.

The Self-fulfilling Prophecy

Each of the major Western religions base their belief systems on scriptures recorded centuries ago. Each teaching predicts more conflict and violence, culminating in one ultimate act of destruction that will be the end of humanity, and likely all life, if not the universe itself. With details that vary from one path to another, this is the story told by Western religions.

I think we are all familiar with the concept of the self-fulfilling prophecy, wherein people who believe strongly in a specific outcome, are inclined to behave in ways that bring into existence what they prophesy. By defining both the desires and fears of Western cultures, the Western exoteric religions have established and nurtured the belief that there is an ongoing battle between good and evil, and that though evil seems to be winning, good will conquer evil in the final scene of Earthly life. When this happens, those whom God judges worthy will be taken away to Heaven for eternity, while the rest will suffer for eternity or be destroyed. Regardless of whether or not Western religions can deliver on the promise of salvation, their history on the planet and their promise of the future, both disclose a legacy of conflict and violence.

For more than a thousand years the world has been living out the self-fulfilling prophecy of Western exoteric religion. Each generation, in the footsteps of Adam and Eve, has learned the power of judgment and constructed a network of polarized concepts, which define the parameters of the reality in which we live.

Just One Thing

On Eckhart Tolle's web site, he writes in an article titled *The One Thing*, "As I was writing *A New Earth*, people would sometimes ask me, 'What is the new book about?' And invariably, my answer would be, 'I only ever write or speak about one thing.' What is that one thing? Spiritual awakening." Can a spiritual awakening occur simply because you read a book? Yes, says Tolle, but only if certain conditions are satisfied.

1) The reader must be ripe to the experience, the mind must be open and not attached to restrictive concepts; what Tolle calls "a readiness to awaken." Tolle points out the increasing number of people who are displaying this readiness.

2) The book itself must convey something beyond the information value of the words. It will have transformational power when the words arise from an awakened consciousness. The book will reach beyond the widely varying interests of the readers to find a common ground in the search for truth.

3) The presentation must be culturally inoffensive so as to appeal to a broad range of readers worldwide.

He closes the article with these thoughts regarding the shift, "Millions are now ready to awaken because spiritual awakening is not an option anymore, but a necessity if humanity and the planet are to survive. Everything is speeding up – the madness, the collective egoic dysfunction, as well as the arising of the new consciousness, the awakening.

"We are running out of time. From the perspective of the ego, that's bad news and will give rise to fear. From a higher perspective, the running out of time is exactly what is needed for the new consciousness to come into this world."

Translucence before Clarity

Satori is a sudden enlightenment, often spoken of in Zen. These experiences frequently occur in an environment that is conducive to higher states of consciousness, such as spiritual retreats or other gatherings of the mystically inclined, but sometimes they happen during the quiet moments of daily existence. In either circumstance, when satori happens in the complete absence of resistance, the ego accepts its illusory nature and withdraws into the background, while the background, which contains all of reality, moves into the forefront of awareness, thus begins the process of liberation. Often, however, when faced with the trials and tribulations of living in duality, the mind will conceptualize satori and define it as a "peak experience," as described by Abraham Maslow. Regardless of what it is called, however, no one is unaffected by such experiences and changes begin taking place that cannot be undone.

Arjuna Ardagh believes that many people all over the world are having enlightenment experiences, then returning to everyday life. He refers to these people, who have been exposed to the light of consciousness, but whose egos are not yet completely clear, as being *translucent*. Coining a noun form of the adjective, he calls these people collectively *translucents*, and with that explanation, the title of his book, *The Translucent Revolution*, becomes easily understandable. The title refers to the same paradigm shift that is the focus of this chapter.

Toward the end of *The Translucent Revolution*, Ardagh talks about the pervasiveness of the shift, "At the same time, every writer, teacher, researcher, and translucent-on-the-street I have spoken with is aware of a countervailing, 'emerging paradigm,' with the potential to transform every sphere of life in every part of the world. The birth pangs of *Homo lucidus* may sometimes cause us to yearn for the familiar, but for most people it is too late. The head of the new human being has pushed through, and its first cries are already in the air. We are riding the crest of a worldwide wave whose consequences are unimaginable, and which holds perhaps the only real basis for optimism for our planet and its inhabitants. We can sense the possibility of a quality of life that has seldom been dreamed of. If we fail to take advantage of this opportunity, our present habits may well destroy us."

Growing Truth in a Shrinking World

Lonny Brown, in *Enlightenment in Our Time,* doesn't talk about 2012, but focuses on the shift in consciousness that he has observed; what one might call a tendency toward awakening. "It's the perennial wisdom. The ancient knowledge. The Single Truth with ten thousand names. Buried and rediscovered yet again, when the hearts of people yearn for the cessation of their needless anguish.

"The world is shrinking, and the word is out once more, and – you might say – not a moment too soon. In the soul of a whole new generation of seekers and celebrators: in a wave of enlightening teachers from every culture; in the eyes of wise old souls, and highly evolved newborn messengers; in the pure, channeled wisdom teachings; in the council circles and sweat lodges…It's the source of the sacred in every culture and conviction: the timeless living spirit emerges and reveals itself in a new way, on a new day, for a new age: Eclectic… Iconoclastic. Electronic. Trans-cultural. Post-Modern. Universal.

"It is time to spiritualize the pulsing global electromagnetic nerve network of our collective intelligence, and realize our essential world civilization. And there's no time to waste, for Mankind and the remaining creatures, and the Earth itself are in immanent peril."

Dire Warnings

Beyond the words of warning from the above authors, clearly, we are in a situation that presents an opportunity, if not a necessity, for drastic and immediate change. Global warming and nuclear proliferation head the popular list of dangers and potential disasters that could result if the future continues on course. Here in the United States, a young, controversial, and inexperienced President faces a worldwide economic disaster, and a war in the Middle East that has been going on in one form or another for at least a thousand years. Only halfway through 2009, many states have declared sovereignty, and there are rumblings of a second civil war.

In the last century, advancements in technology and communications have turned the world into a very small place. Like it or not, however, it is not really our world; the world is truly an organism unto itself. In the same way that we are, in a larger sense, expressions of the whole of existence, we are also part of the Earth. We may be good citizens of our country, our neighborhood, our religion, and our family, but if the show is to continue, we must learn to identify with a larger view of reality and act as citizens of the universe. It is no longer profitable to the world for the members of any culture to declare their own superiority in any way, including, militarily, politically, economically, ethically, and spiritually. The imperialism of Western religion and the cultures they represent, has placed the world in imminent danger. The world has grown too small to be divided, and many intelligent people are coming to believe that it is time to become and live as One or die.

A Brief Summary

The *Preface* opened with a statement that this is a book about truth, and is designed to question our assumptions about reality and existence. In one way or another, most of the book has been about this task. A secondary purpose of the book is to focus attention on the shift to awakened consciousness that is taking place in a growing number of people at this time. Throughout the book the awakened nondual perspective has been emphasized; the movement and timing of this shift is covered primarily in this last chapter.

In *Part I*, *Introductions*, the first chapter introduced Sophia Perennis and the idea of the ineffable perennial wisdom. We talked about Western religion and how it has weaknesses that prevent it from satisfying the spiritual needs of modern rational humans. We discovered poorly recorded, outdated, ethical doctrines that function due to the pressures of the desire and fear that we allow them to impose on our lives. In chapter two we explored some experiences of the individual who wrote this book.

The reality that we experience is based on *Polarities*, and that is the topic of *Part II*. It is the recognition of the self as an individual that creates duality, a reality based on opposing concepts. At the root of our dualistic reality is nonduality, which is the platform from which duality arises when judgments are made. We talked about the differences between logos and mythos as functions of culture and perspectives on truth. We broke down religion into esoteric and exoteric and discussed these disparate views of spirituality. We found that good and evil are not inherently found in reality but are part of our cognitive structure. Finally, we considered that perhaps our sense of controlling the direction of our lives through free will may very well be an illusion.

We began *Part III*, which is about *Processes*, with a look at Western religion through the eyes of a thinking child, beginning with the Garden of Eden myth and Augustine's interpretation of that story, from which emerged the doctrine of Original Sin. In this light we looked at aspects of religious education, we saw myth being taken as fact, and we considered the child's image of God based on the Garden of Eden and other Bible stories. In chapter nine, we took a "hit and miss" overview of various spiritual paths, and chapter ten entertained the idea that it is our concept of time that stands between our individual selves and the eternal timeless One.

Time is the factor that allows the ego to separate the present into past and future, thereby moving the attention from the present moment to mental processes, either memories coded as our past or anticipations coded as future. In order to realize Oneness, we must also realize the nature of multiplicity, and it is this mind created ego image of an independent self that we investigate in chapter eleven. We explored views of the individual as a physical entity, as a personality, as a mental image, and as an illusion. We considered the deconstruction of the ego using self-enquiry, and spontaneous disillusion through trauma and the aging process on our way to *Part IV, Oneness*.

When you are conditioned to think in terms of self and other, the concept of unity looks like individuals united in some way, such as marital union, a labor union, United Way, etc. In chapter twelve we talked about a primary unity that is transcendent. We looked at unity from a psychological perspective, philosophically, the view of quantum physics, and from New Age nonduality. Where there is resistance to *what is*, however, the illusion of the individual will persist, and transcendent unity will not be realized until the awakening or enlightenment.

This subject has been a running theme throughout the book and finally, spiritual awakening is the focus of lucky chapter thirteen. The very word awakening reveals the analogy that we first used to approached this ineffable subject. We played with variations on the waking from the dream analogy, wherein, life is envisioned as a dream in which we are trapped until we somehow become aware that we are asleep to a larger reality. Douglas Harding described his enlightenment experience with the analogy of having no head, and we discussed one of my favorite analogies for awakening, the stereogram.

We listed some of the perceived qualities of enlightenment, and considered another psychological view on awakening. The subject of teachers and teachings finished the chapter as we question how, from the awakened position, there can be a separation between teacher and student? When Oneness is realized, the teacher, the student, and the path that was followed, all dissolve as would the dream from which you have just awakened. The teacher who brings Awakening cannot be other than the One dreamer. We are characters in a dream of suffering, unaware of the enlightened universe all around us.

All this has brought us to *Part V* and *Conclusions*, where we are discussing this shift, this wave of enlightenment that seems to be striving for and achieving some sort of critical mass, such as the "hundredth monkey" syndrome, at which point an evolutionary switch will flip and in a very short time, the whole species of wise man, *Homo sapiens*, will evolve into a race of enlightened beings. At the core of the myriad spiritual paths available to humanity in the twenty-first century, Sophia Perennis, wherever it is found, by whatever name, is the thread of truth that runs through all spiritual teachings, it is what always points to the truth of nonduality.

New Beginnings

We have covered a multitude of diverse subjects and have summarized them in the previous section. In bringing this book to a close, perhaps the best way to conclude is to return to the original premises. The two premises that I hope are well supported by this book are:

1.) Western religions generally welcome converts to their belief systems. Because of the exclusive nature of the doctrines, however, those who believe otherwise are viewed with suspicion. If only one system is right, other belief systems, therefore, must all be wrong, and perhaps even evil. These belief systems grow out of an antiquated view of life that is at odds with much of what we understand about the world today. All of these systems are plagued with a history of war and violence that reaches into modern times with modern weapons capable of destroying the planet and everything on it. Having people who are willing to kill for their beliefs is bad enough, but having people who are hoping to die for their religion is worse. It is time to abandon the violent, exclusive, worldview of Western religion and adopt more inclusive belief systems that allow people to live in proximity and harmony.

2.) The pace of change in our world has accelerated to the extent that we can no longer deny that we have reached the point of chaos. Many countries now have nuclear weapons and world politics are quite volatile. The ecosystem is under great strain as the Earth is subject to natural forces while at the same time being pillaged by the needs of a growing mass of humanity. Planetary and social systems in a state of chaos are very sensitive to small changes in the environment; a seemingly insignificant event could lead to the cascading failure of cultural and environmental systems throughout the world. Meanwhile, the foreboding prophecies of Western religions hang in the minds of a populace that is angry, afraid, and confused.

Within this unstable framework, however, there is a new paradigm emerging as more and more people are shifted to higher states of consciousness and ultimately to awakening. The shift of consciousness that we have talked about in this book, is moving toward a new consensus that points, not to more violence and destruction, but to unity as the only workable solution to the current state of humanity.

If the ideas discussed in this book seem nonsensical, offensive, or threatening in any way, read it again, because what we have shared in these pages is exceedingly important. The reading of this book represents a step in your spiritual unfolding; I implore you to take another, and another.

On the other hand, if the ideas presented here resonate with any part of your being, then to some extent you have already engaged the shift and the transformation has begun. It has begun at least as a process of preparation, which can take some time as resistance fades and energy gathers. The shift itself will occur outside of time as you realize that enlightenment has always been the case, and that beyond *what is* in the present moment, there was never anything to seek.

Any ego that is seeking spiritual truth will likely come to believe that enlightenment will make it feel better, improve its image, or complete it in some way. Inevitably, the question will be asked, "Is there anything 'I' can do to further the process of awakening?" This is a difficult question to answer because it spans a gap that the ego cannot comprehend, let alone cross of its own volition. If the ego, the you that you think you are, can do anything at all, it is, as much as possible, to be open to new perspectives, suspend judgments, stay in the present moment, and to recognize, follow, and surrender to the natural impulse toward transcendence as best you can. Most of all, whenever it is appropriate and possible to do so, chose to be happy.

Regardless of whether you consider yourself a seeker of truth or you are committed and loyal to some specific belief system, you have engaged this book. It is your conditioning that has placed it in your hands; ultimately, there are no mistakes. If you have read this book with an open mind, then these words and the considerations we have explored are now part of your conditioning as well. If a part of you is moved in the direction of nonduality, do not be afraid, it's a natural thing, welcome to the shift, and by all means, carry on.

Index

Bibliography

Adyashanti, *Spontaneous Awakening*, audio recording, Sounds True, Boulder, CO, 2005.

Adyashanti, *The Impact of Awakening; Excerpts from the Teachings of Adyashanti*, Open Gate Publishing, Los Gatos, CA 2005.

American Museum of Natural History, Internet article, http://www.amnh.org/exhibitions/einstein/time/revolution.php, 2009.

Answers.com Online Dictionary, http://www.answers.com/time?gwp=11&ver=2.4.0.651&method=3, 2008.

Ardagh, Arjuna, *The Transparent Revolution: How People Just Like You Are WAKING UP and CHANGING the World,* New World Library, Novato, CA, 2005.

Armstrong, Karen, *The Battle for God: A History of Fundamentalism*, Random House Ballantine, New York, NY, 2001.

Bohm, David, *Unfolding Meaning; A Weekend of Dialogue with David Bohm*, Routledge & Kegan Paul, Inc., New York, NY, 1985

Braden, Gregg, *Fractal Time; The Secret of 2012 and a New World Age*, Hay House, Inc., Carlsbad, CA, 2009.

Britannica Concise Encyclopedia, online encyclopedia entry, http://www.encyclopedia.com/doc/1B1-383282.html, 2009.

Brown, Lonny J., *Enlightenment in Our Time; The Perennial Wisdom in the New Millennium*, www.BookLocker.com/LonnyBrown , www.LonnyBrown.com, Enlightenment Projects, Peterborough, NH, 2001.

Campbell, Joseph, *Mythology and the Individual*, audio recording, HighBridge Company, St. Paul, MN, 1996.

Campbell, Joseph, *The Power of Myth*, audio recording, Apostrophe S Productions, HighBridge Company, St Paul, MN 1988.

Campbell, Joseph, *Thou Art That; Transforming Religious Metaphor*, Edited by Kennedy, Eugene, New World Library, Novato, CA, 2001.

Capra, Fritjof, *The Tao of Physics: An Exploration of the Parallels between Modern Physics and Eastern Mysticism*, Shambhala Publications, Inc., Boulder, CO, 1975.

Catholic Online Encyclopedia, http://www.newadvent.org/cathen/, 2009.

Christian Neuroscience Society, *Quantum Physics and Free Will; A Misguided Concept*, Internet article, http://www.cneuroscience.org/Topics/Will/Quantum_Free_Will.htm, 2008.

Claxton, Guy, *Hare Brain, Tortoise Mind; How Intelligence Increases When You Think Less.* HarperCollins, New York, NY, 1997.

Cook, David, transcript of an interview with Deborah Caldwell for BeliefNet, *Islamic Apocalypse?*, http://www.beliefnet.com/Faiths/Islam/2003/03/Islamic-Apocalypse.aspx, 2009.

Davies, Paul, *The Mind of God; The Scientific Basis for a Rational World*, Touchstone, New York, NY, 1992.

Dawkins, Richard, *The God Delusion*, Houghton Mifflin Company, New York, NY, 2006.

Dennett, Daniel C. , *Breaking the Spell: Religion as a Natural Phenomenon*, The Penguin Group, New York, NY, 2006.

Einstein, Albert, *Relativity, the Special and General Theory*, Crown Publishers, Inc., New York, NY, 1961.

Erhman, Bart, *Misquoting Jesus: The Story Behind Who Changed the Bible and Why,* HarperCollins, New York, NY, 2007.

Erikson, Erik H., *Identity: Youth and Crisis.* Norton, New York, NY, 1968.

Folger, Tim, *Newsflash: Time May Not Exist*, http://discovermagazine.com/2007/jun/in-no-time, 2008.

Freke, Timothy, & Gandy, Peter, *The Laughing Jesus; Religious Lies and Gnostic Wisdom*, Random House, Three Rivers Press, New York, NY, 2005.

Grof, Stanislav, *Psychology of the Future: Lessons From Modern Consciousness Research*, SUNY Press, New York, NY, 2000.

Harding, Douglas E., *On Having No Head: Zen and the Rediscovery of the Obvious*, Inner Directions, Carlsbad, CA 2004.

Harris, Sam, *The End of Faith: Religion, Terror, and the Future of Reason*, W. W. Norton & Company, Inc., New York, NY 2004.

Hartong , Leo , *Awakening to the Dream; The Gift of Lucid Living,* NonDuality Press, Salisbury, UK, 2003.

Hawking, Steven, *A Brief History of Time; From the Big Bang to Black Holes*, Bantam Books, New York, NY, 1988.

Hay, Louise, *You can Heal Your Life*, Hay House, San Diego, CA, 1999.

Heylighen, Francis, *Punctuated Equilibrium*, Internet article (1999), http://pespmc1.vub.ac.be/Punctueq.html, 2009.

Hicks, Esther & Hicks, Jerry, *Ask and It Is Given; Learning to Manifest Your Desires*, Hay House, Carlsbad, CA, 2004.

Hicks, Esther & Hicks, Jerry, *Introductory Audio,* MP3 Download, available at http://www.abraham-hicks.com/lawofattractionsource/mp3downloads.php, 2009

Hitchens, Christopher, *god is not Great: How Religion Poisons Everything*, Hachette Book Group USA, New York, NY, 2007.

Huxley, Aldous, *The Perennial Philosophy; An Interpretation of the Great Mystics, East and West*, HarperCollins Perennial Classic edition, New York, NY 2004.

Joseph, Peter, *Zeitgeist*, www.zeitgeistmovie.com, 2009.

Katz, Jerry, *One; Essential Writings on Nonduality*, Sentient Publications, Boulder, CO, 2007.

Kersschot, Jan, *This Is It; The Nature of Oneness*, Watkins Press, London, 2004.

King, Godfré Ray, *Unveiled Mysteries*, Bibliobazaar, Charleston, SC, 2007, orig. 1934.

Krishnamurti, Jiddu & Bohm, David, *The Ending of Time*, HarperCollins, New York, NY, 1985.

Lao-Tzu, *Tao te Ching*, translated by Brian Browne Walker, St. Martin Press, New York, NY, 1995.

Laszlo, Ervin, *The Chaos Point; The World at the Crossroads*, Hampton Roads Publishing Company, Inc. Charlottesville, VA, 2006.

Laughlin, Paul Alan & Jackson, Glenna S., *Remedial Christianity; What Every Believer Should Know about the Faith, but Probably Doesn't*, Polebridge Press, Santa Rosa, CA, 2000.

Laughlin, Paul Alan, *Getting Oriented; What Every Christian Should Know about Eastern Religions, but Probably Doesn't,* Polebridge Press, Santa Rosa, CA, 2005.

Libet, Benjamin, *Mind Time: The Temporal Factor in Consciousness,* Harvard University Press, Cambridge, MA, 2005.

Loy, David, *Nonduality: A Study in Comparative Philosophy,* Humanity Books, Amherst, NY, 1999.

Maharshi, Ramana, *Talks with Ramana Maharshi; On Realizing Abiding Peace and Happiness,* Inner Directions Publishing, Carlsbad, CA, 2001.

Maslow, Abraham, *The Farther Reaches of Human Nature.* Viking Press, New York, NY, 1971.

McKenna, Jed, *Spiritual Enlightenment: The Damnedest Thing,* Wisefool Press, location not given, 2002.

McKenna, Terrence & McKenna, Dennis, *The Invisible Landscape: Mind, Hallucinations and the I Ching,* HarperCollins, New York, NY, 1975.

NASA, various Internet press releases, http://www.nasa.gov/home/index.html, 2008.

Ontario Consultants on Religious Tolerance, various Internet articles, http://www.religioustolerance.org/isl_intr.htm, 2008.

Ray Kurzweil, *The Singularity is Near - An Amazing Future,* Internet article, http://singularity.com/themovie/future.php, 2008.

Renz , Karl, *The Myth of Enlightenment; Seeing Through the Illusion of Separation,* Inner Directions, Carlsbad, CA, 2005.

Roberts, Bernadette, *The Path to No-Self; Life at the Center,* SUNY Press, Albany, NY 1991.

Rood, Rick, *The Problem of Evil: How can a Good God Allow Evil?* Internet article, Leadership University Probe Ministries, http://www.leaderu.com/orgs/probe/docs/evil.html, 2008.

Russell, Peter, *A Singularity in Time,* in *The Mystery of 2012; Predictions, Prophecies & Possibilities,* Sounds True, Boulder, CO, 2007.

Śaranam, Śankara, *God Without Religion; Questioning Centuries of Accepted Truths,* The Pranayama Institute, Inc., Columbus, NM, 2005.

Schopenhauer, Arthur, *Short Dialogue on the Indestructibility of Our True Being by Death, Essays of Schopenhauer,* eBooks@Adelaide, 2004.

Schuon, Frithjof, *The Transcendent Unity of Religions;,* Quest Books, Wheaton, IL, 1984.

Schuon, Frithjof, *What is Sophia Perennis; According to Frithjof Schuon,* Internet article: http://www.sophia-perennis.com/introduction-eng.htm, 2009

Sitchin, Zecharia, *The Earth Chronicles,* Avon Books, New York, NY, 1976.

Sobottka, Stanley, *A Course in Consciousness,* Internet book, http://faculty.virginia.edu/consciousness, 2009.

Socrates, in Plato, *Dialogues, Apology,* Greek philosopher in Athens.

Sounds True, *The Mystery of 2012; Predictions, Prophecies & Possibilities,* Author, Boulder, CO, compiled 2007.

Stieger, Brad, *In My Soul I Am Free; The Incredible Paul Twitchell Story,* Lancer Press, 1968.

Strawson, Galen, *Free Will,* Routledge Encyclopedia of Philosophy, http://www.rep.routledge.com/article/V014, 2009.

Talbot, Michael, *Mysticism and the New Physics,* Penguin Putnam, New York, NY, 1993.

The Bible, Old and New Testament.

The Church of Critical Thinking, *Planet X Nibiru Projected Orbital Return 2012 AD*, Internet article, http://churchofcriticalthinking.org/planetx.html, 2009.

The History Channel, *God vs. Satan*, video, http://shop.history.com/detail.php?p=74013&v=All, 2009.

Tolle, Eckhart, *A New Earth; Awakening to Your Life's Purpose*, audio recording, Penguin Audio, New York, NY, 2005.

Tolle, Eckhart, *The One Thing*, Internet article, http://eckharttolle.com/a_new_earth, 2009.

Tolle, Eckhart, *The Power of Now; A Guide to Spiritual Enlightenment.* , New World Library, Novato, CA, 1999.

Tolle, Eckhart, *Stillness Speaks*, New World Library, Novato, CA, and Namaste Publishing, Vancouver, Canada, 2003

Tolle, Eckhart, *Through the Open Door to the Vastness of Your True Being*, audio recording, Sounds True, Boulder, CO, 2006.

Trasi Nitin, The International Conference of Knowledge and East-West Transitions, December 2000, Internet article , *What is Enlightenment?*, http://www.geocities.com/nitin_trasi/wie.html, 2008.

Ullman, Robert & Reichenberg-Ullman, Judyth, *Mystics, Masters, Saints, and Sages*, Conari Press, Boston, MA 2001.

Vitale, Joe & Hew Len, Ihaleakala, *Zero Limits: The Secret Hawaiian System for Wealth, Health, Peace and More*, John Wiley & Sons, Inc., Hoboken, NJ, 2007.

Vitale, Joe, *The Attractor Factor: 5 Easy steps for Creating Wealth (and anything else) from the inside out*, John Wiley & Sons, Inc., Hoboken, NJ, 2005.

Wade, Jenny, *Changes of Mind; A Holonomic Theory of the Evolution of Consciousness*, SUNY Press, New York, NY, 1996.

Watts, Alan, *Out of Your Mind*, audio recording, Sounds True, San Anselmo, CA, 2004.

Watts, Alan, *The Book On the Taboo Against Knowing Who You Are*, Random House, New York, NY, 1966.

Watts, Alan, *The Wisdom of Insecurity; A Message for an Age of Anxiety*, Random House of Canada Limited, Toronto, 1951.

Wilber, Ken, *No Boundary; Eastern and Western Approaches to Personal Growth*, Shambhala Publications, Inc., Boston, MA, 2001.

Wise, Russ, *The Deception of Eckhart Tolle*, The Christian Information Ministries, Internet article, http://www.christianinformation.org/article.asp?artID=122, 2009.

Recommended Reading

The books that are listed in this section are some of the books that I have read over the past ten years or more. In order to give full detailed reviews of them I would want to read them all over. The criteria used for making these recommendations, however, will be based on my recollections of the books and a quick scan to refresh the memory.

Not everything in the following list is based on nonduality. Of those that are nondual there is considerable overlap as these teachings all stem from Sophia Perennis. The distinct flavor of each nondual path is determined by shifting emphasis and by the inevitable distortion that occurs when the unspeakable truth is conceptualized to make it palatable to the mind. It is the mind, after all, which must make sense out of books such as these. For the convenience of the diverse minds who will read these words I have attempted to structure this list into categories that make some sort of sense.

Someone at the height of financial success will require a different approach than one who has just had a near death experience. Those who have followed a Western theology most of their lives will see nonduality from a different view than will long-time seekers. What we are dealing with is different ways of trying to get the mind to accept a truth that is incomprehensible because it is too simple to be expressed with language or even thought. With that in mind we begin with a level of teachings directed at those who are strongly feeling the pull toward transcendence.

Hardcore Nonduality

The authors in this group write straightforward nonduality. The teachings are direct and they do not coddle the ego nor spend a lot of effort trying to calm the egoic mind or lead it toward enlightenment. These teachings are not directed toward improving the egoic self, but if you are sincerely interested in waking up, these books may be helpful.

Bear in mind that many of them openly admit that the individual can do nothing to bring about enlightenment, I guess that sounds like something of a paradox. If you are going to read this type of book, however, I suggest you learn to deal with paradox, not as a state of conflict, but as a state of equilibrium or balance in the universe. Another thing to remember is that the less you engage the judging mind, the better off you will be.

Many of the books listed here are written in dialogue or Q&A style designed to address the questions that many seekers have about waking up. Several of the authors in this group are published by non-Duality Press out of the UK, where there seems to be a growing neo-Advaita movement.

Adams, Robert (1928–1997)	Adams was a student of Ramana Maharshi, and a highly respected teacher from the Advaita Vedanta lineage of Nisargadatta Maharaj. More information about Robert Adams can be found at a web site maintained in his name at http://www.robertadamsinfinityinstitute.org/. Adams was not a prolific writer but much of his written and recorded material is available through this site. Most consider *Silence of the Heart,* a compilation first published the year he died, to be his magnum opus.
Adamson, "Sailor" Bob	A student of Nisargadatta Maharaj, Adamson is considered an important figure in the nonduality movement. Adamson teaches out of Australia, and has written two short books that are almost entirely Q&A. His ideas are certainly Advaita, but having read both, *What's Wrong with Right Now; unless you think about it?* and *Presence-Awareness; Just This and Nothing More*, I personally do not care for the Q&A technique nor his particular presentation. He seems to have a significant following, however, and he may be just the perfect teacher for you. Information is available at, http://members.iinet.net.au/~adamson7/. You may also purchase books, as well as audio and video recordings.
Adyashanti	Born Steven Gray in 1962 near San Francisco, in his late teens he began studying Zen. After fifteen years of study, he became enlightened and began to teach. In addition to speaking engagements, he has authored books and has recorded talks available. Adyashanti has a very affable style and a soothing voice. His direct teaching is Zen-like but even simpler. His web site is http://www.adyashanti.org/.

Balsekar, Ramesh S.	He was born in India in 1917, and was drawn, even as a child to nondual thinking. After retiring as President of the Bank of India in 1977, Balsekar met and developed a close relationship with Nisargadatta Maharaj. His enlightenment experience is nicely summed up on his web site, "The total understanding that 'no one does anything' happened in 1979." His official web site is found at http://www.rameshbalsekar.com/default.asp.
Carse, David	This Vermont farmer/carpenter/building contractor begins his book on nonduality with a disclaimer of sorts, One single spaced page titled *The Fine Print* begins his book, *Perfect Brilliant Stillness; Beyond the Individual Self.* Carse writes: "There are many books out there that will help you to live a better life, become a better person, and evolve and grow to realize your full potential as a spiritual being.
	"This is not one of them.
	"This book will tell you that these ideas are absurd, because it's quite obvious that neither you nor anything else has ever existed."
Crowley, Gary	A simple truth expressed simply in one small book, fewer than 100 pages, double-spaced, sum up this authors perspective of a nondual reality. *From Here to Here, Turning Toward Enlightenment* is a joy to read with good examples from different perspectives. I look forward to the next book from this author. His web site is at http://garycrowley.com/.
Foster, Jeff	With three books to his credit in as many years, Foster is one of several neo-Advaita teachers out of the UK. His message is that seeking is over, there is nothing to seek. Appreciate *what is*, because that is really all we have. I have read *Beyond Awakening; The End of the Spiritual Search*, and its nondual premise, that there is no individual to be enlightened, is nicely presented in

various formats from Q&A to poetry. His teaching is very simple and clearly outlined on his web site, http://www.lifewithoutacentre.com/, which is also the title of his first book.

Gill, Nathan	Another proponent of neo-Advaita, Gill has little regard for the needs of any individual including himself. At http://www.nathangill.com/, on the "About the Author" page of his web site, there is only a picture of Gill hoeing dirt and the following text, "Nathan was born in 1960 and lives in rural England, working as a gardener." He first came to my attention as the writer of an article titled *Clarity*, which is included in his book, *Already Awake*. I have also read *Being; The Bottom Line*, and both books are done in Q&A style but filled with humor.
Greven, John	A Foreword by Sailor Bob Adamson clearly identifies the ideas in this author's one book, "*Oneness; The Destination You Never Left*," as Advaita. His book is fewer than 100 pages, it is simple and concise. The individual falls to the wayside with the Advaita teachings and Greven offers no personal information on his web site, http://www.onenessjustthat.com/.
Hartong, Leo	I have read one of Hartong's two books, *Awakening to the Dream; The gift of lucid living*. Perhaps more than most in this group, he considers the view of the individual mind and its love of a good story. In this book he includes his "personal" story, growing up in post-WWII Europe, and the counterculture of the 1960's. He maintains a web site and sells his books at, http://www.awakeningtothedream.com/.
Hillig, Chuck	A former US Naval officer, he held several positions in the field of psychotherapy prior to writing seven books on spirituality and psychology. Best known for his "Enlightenment Quartet", I have read only one of the

four, *Looking for God; Seeing the Whole in One*, a book that is written around a one inch hole that runs cover to cover through the middle of the book. It is a simple book about nonduality suitable for children. His web site is http://www.chuckhillig.com/.

Kersschot, Jan   With five spiritually oriented books to his credit, Kersschot is a medical doctor who practices in Belgium. I have read *This is It; The Nature of Oneness*, of which two thirds consists of interviews with well known authors and teachers of nonduality. More than the interviews, I enjoyed the first part that expressed his own views, and will read his other books as time permits. His web site offers information on both nondual philosophy and his medical practice at http://www.kersschot.com/.

Klein, Jean   Born in Eastern Europe, biographical information
(1916–??)   regarding Dr. Klein is somewhat scarce. Highly influenced in his youth by René Guénon, as a young man he traveled to India to study Advaita. Awakening occurred in 1955 and he began teaching in 1960. I read *I AM*, a small book in Q&A format. I found various links to his web site, http://www.jeanklein.com, but they did not connect.

Krishnamurti,   I have read a number of articles by UG, and one of his
U. G.   books, *The Mystique of Enlightenment*, in which he tells
(1918–2007)   his own very interesting story. Though most of his works are published in dialogue format, I still find him quite entertaining. He often speaks of his own enlightenment experience as "the calamity." His web site, http://ugkrishnamurti.com/, is still working but has not been updated since December of 2007.

Lake, Gina   My first encounter with Gina Lake was as a channel for a group of nonphysical entities going by the name of Theo. I had never done anything like that before and I thought it would be good research material. After talking with her, and Theo, I read her book, *Radical Happiness; A Guide to Awakening*, and enjoyed it quite a lot. The "radical happiness" is the ever-present happiness that is not dependent on circumstances; it is the happiness of awakening. She has eight books out and a newsletter that she and her husband write, available at http://radicalhappiness.com/.

Maharaj,
Nisargadatta
(1897–1981)

Born to poor Indian peasant farmers, he became a successful businessman selling tobacco in the nearby city. Though not an educated man, he has taught many who have become highly respected teachers, a few of whom are named here. His book, *I Am That,* is "a modern spiritual classic" and should be considered a "must read" by any sincere seeker. His many books, audio, and video recordings, are available at the web site, http://www.maharajnisargadatta.com/.

Maharshi,
Ramana
(1879 –1950)

In modern times, the name of this sage is synonymous with traditional Indian Advaita Vedanta. On the cover of *"Talks with Ramana Maharshi"* Ken Wilber proclaims that *"Talks* is the living voice of the greatest sage of the twentieth century." A big book of over five hundred pages, like most of the many books by or about him, is in Q&A format. Information is available at http://www.sriramanamaharshi.org/.

Nadeen,
Satyam

This author and teacher is not the stereotypic "holy man," as awakening and the writing of his first book, *Onions to Pearls*, occurred while he was in federal prison for drug dealing. His second book, *From Seekers to Finders*, explores the myths and realities of enlightenment. I read this one and found his informal presentation easy to follow and quite clear. He talks about enlightenment as the shift from seeking truth to finding truth. He has written only two books, but seems dedicated to his teaching practice out of Georgia and

Costa Rica. Details are available at his web site, http://www.satyamnadeen.com/.

Parsons, Tony	At the center of this UK based author's teaching is the idea that enlightenment is constantly present and the invitation to awaken is always available. Born in London in 1933, at the age of twenty he awoke to his true nature. His material is straightforward and simple. Of his two books, *As It Is* is almost half dialogues and *Invitation to Awaken* is virtually all dialogue. His extensive speaking schedule in Europe and the UK, books, and recordings are available for purchase, and free downloads are at, http://www.theopensecret.com/.
Renz, Karl	Originally from Germany, Renz studied agriculture before focusing on art and music. In the late 70's, he had a profound shift in consciousness that awakened him to the realization of immortality and dissolved the concept of a separate self. Since the 1990s, he has responded to numerous invitations to hold dialogues and meetings around the world. His web site, at http://www.karlrenz.com/index.html promotes his art and music as well as his writing on nonduality.
Sobottka, Stanley	This author is an emeritus professor of physics at the University of Virginia. His book, *A Course in Consciousness* is an online document that is free, not protected by copyright, and the author encourages distribution of this work. The book is an ongoing work that has been around since 2000 and is updated often. This marvelous nondual scientific work is available at http://faculty.virginia.edu/consciousness.
Watts, Alan (1915–1973)	Watts was introduced to nonduality via Zen during his youth in England. In 1938 he moved to the US and made it home. Of his over two dozen books, I have read six or seven, he also has recorded lectures available of which I have four volumes. He combines obscure tidbits

of spiritual information and interesting anecdotes to weave a nondual tapestry that is life itself. The "Alan Watts Archive" is an internet resource site maintained by Watt's family at http://www.alanwatts.com/.

Wei Wu Wei (1895 –1986)	This author was born Terence Gray, to a prominent Irish family, and raised outside of Cambridge, England. He was well educated, including studies at Oxford. He led a full life of diverse experience, which included studying with spiritual masters of the Far East, before, at the age of 63, publishing the first of eight books on nonduality under the pseudonym Wei Wu Wei. All of these books are still in print from Sentient Publication, LLC. I have read *Open Secret* and his approach to nonduality is not for the faint of heart. This is a book that you will either love or hate. If you get it, you will applaud his cleverness; if you don't get it, it will seem like nonsense or insanity. More information, excerpts from the books, articles, and more are available at his web site http://www.weiwuwei.8k.com/index.html.

Mainstream Western Religion

As there are plenty of books that wholeheartedly endorse religion as a means to peace and happiness, in order to be "fair and balanced," many of the names you will find in this list of authors will question or outright oppose Western religion as a way of expressing the spiritual aspect of life.

Armstrong, Karen	*The Battle for God* is a Bestseller from an ex-nun turned author who is critical of fundamentalism. This is a highly detailed historical account of the rise of fundamentalism in Western religions and the cultural threats that accompany these religious beliefs. She believes that mythos has outlived its usefulness and that in modern culture it is dangerous to interpret scripture literally. Though she has a presence on the Internet, I was a bit surprised that I was unable to find a web site dedicated exclusively to her work.
Borg, Marcus	In *Reading the Bible Again for the First Time* a religious scholar talks about the Bible as myth. *The Lost Gospel Q* is a reconstruction of fragments of documents found over the past 150 years. It is considered the first gospel. A web site on Borg and his latest book can be found at http://www.aportraitofjesus.org/index.shtml
Ehrman, Bart	An ivy league religious education turns a born again teenager into an agnostic scientist. In *Misquoting Jesus: The Story Behind Who Changed the Bible and Why*, the author describes his study of textual criticism as it applies to how the Bible has changed over time and why. After years of studying the Bible and its origins, Ehrman concludes that there is little in the modern Bible to justify the belief that it is the inerrant word of God. Information about the author, and his two Bestseller books, this one and *God's Problem: How the Bible Fails to Answer Our most Important Question – Why do we suffer?*, can be found at the web site http://bartdehrman.com/.

Freke, Timothy & Gandy, Peter	*The Laughing Jesus: Religious Lies and Gnostic Wisdom* looks at Jesus as the hero of a Gnostic myth. Examining the scriptures from this perspective illuminates an entirely different view of what Christianity is really about. They authors clearly show Gnosticism, from which Christianity developed, as a nondual teaching. The book uses the old adage, "Don't throw out the baby with the bathwater," as an analogy for cleaning up our spiritual perspective. This is an interesting read with lots of humor. I found little information on Gandy, but there is a web site for Freke at http://www.timothyfreke.com/.
Harris, Sam	Like others listed here, Harris has expressed a concern with the recent growth of Western fundamentalism. In his Bestseller, *The End of Faith: Religion, Terror, and the Future of Reason*, he implicates religious moderates as complicit in the rise of terrorism. He convincingly portrays all Western religion as dangerous myth if not a full-out delusion. Information on Harris and his books can be found at http://www.samharris.org/.
Laughlin, Paul Alan	*Remedial Christianity: What Every Believer Should Know about the Faith, but Probably Doesn't* was written by a Christian minister and former chairman of Philosophy and Religion at Otterbein College in Ohio who favors a more open look at Christianity.
	In his second book, *Getting Oriented: What Every Christian Should Know about Eastern Religion, but Probably Doesn't*, he focuses on the integration of Eastern monistic teachings as a way to achieve a more enlightened Christianity. His web site, which is at, http://laughlinonline.net/homepaulblue.html, shows a strong Eastern bent.

Renard, Gary R.	*The Disappearance of the Universe* is a nicely written approach to nonduality based on *A Course in Miracles*. It is written as a dialogue between the author and two ascended masters who discuss "illusions, past lives, religion, sex, politics, and the miracles of forgiveness." It is a rather long book but it was well worth the effort. His web site is http://www.garyrenard.com/.
Roberts, Bernadette	This author tells how she found the truth of nonduality in Christianity, not in the traditional teachings of the Church, but as a Christian Contemplative. *The Path to No Self: Life at the Center* tells of her spiritual journey, and offers a rare look at a Christian perspective about which the Church has little to say. She only gives retreats once a year. A web site is maintained on her behalf at http://www.bernadettesfriends.blogspot.com/
S, Ancharya	This author wrote *The Christ Conspiracy: The Greatest Story Ever Sold*, which examines the roots and development of Christianity as a conglomerate of ideas borrowed from older myths with timing that is based in astrology. This book is more a critique of Christianity than a promotion of nondualism, but if you happen to be questioning your Christian beliefs, much information is available in this book and her web site that may help you, http://www.truthbeknown.com/.
Saranam, Sankara	After a period of intense study, Saranam saw how the human sense of identity manifests. His multi award winning book, *God Without Religion*, grew out of a nonreligious view of the relationship between God and man. This is an engaging book, which tells how religion disempowers humanity. From the introduction, "If there is a useful purpose served by religions that continue to disempower any portion of the human race, it can only be in inspiring us to prevent history from repeating itself." His web site is http://www.pranayama.org/

Schuon, Frithjof (1907–1998)	*The Transcendent Unity of Religions* is the first major work by Schuon who went on to become one of the most important religious scholars of the twentieth century. This is a good introduction to the Traditionalist Philosophy for those who enjoy scholarly writing. His estate continues to run the web site, http://www.frithjof-schuon.com/start.htm, and his extensive writings on sophia perennis are available.
Smith, Huston	Born in China, the child of missionaries, Smith had the opportunity to study Eastern religion in its native habitat. Though primarily self taught, he is highly respected in academic circles as an authority in comparative religion. His book, *The World's Religions*, is a extraordinary reference work by one of the greatest religious scholars of our time. His Web site is http://www.hustonsmith.net/.
Watts, Alan (1915–1973)	On the back cover of *Myth and Ritual in Christianity* is a descriptive excerpt from the book's Prologue: "Our main object will be to describe one of the most incomparably beautiful myths that has ever flowered from the mind of man, or from the unconscious processes which shape it and which are in some sense more than man....This is, furthermore, to be a description and not a history of Christian Mythology...After description, we shall attempt an interpretation of the myth along the general lines of the *philosophia perennis*, in order to bring out the truly catholic or universal character of the symbols, and to share the delight of discovering a fountain of wisdom in a realm where so many have long ceased to expect anything but a desert of platitudes." Amen.

Philosophy

What is offered here is but a small sampling from a diverse field of knowledge. This particular list includes academic, spiritual, and what might be called "lay" perspectives. While they may not fall into the "philosophy of religion" category, the examples listed here do emphasize religion from various perspectives.

Campbell, Joseph (1904–1987)	Edited by Eugene Kennedy, *Thou Art That*, is a compilation of newly released work by a beloved mythologist, writer, teacher, and storyteller. My enjoyment of Campbell comes mainly from two old sets of audio recordings (on cassette) that I think are much better than the book. *The Power of Myth* with Bill Moyers is the audio from the PBS series of the same name. *Mythology and the Individual* is a series of Campbell's early lectures. The web site of the Joseph Campbell Foundation is at http://www.jcf.org/new/index.php.
Dawkins, Richard	British ethnologist and evolutionary biologist, Dawkins is also an outspoken atheist. *The God Delusion* is the latest of ten books by this author. In it Dawkins contends that a supernatural creator almost certainly does not exist and that faith qualifies as a delusion – as a fixed false belief. Information and downloads are available at http://richarddawkins.net/
Dennett, Daniel C.	Dennett is an American philosopher who has been writing books since 1969. His latest work, *Breaking the Spell: Religion as a Natural Phenomenon*, is an examination of religious beliefs as a pervasive ingredient of human culture and possibly human nature. Dennett approaches his premise deftly from different angles as he explores the reasons that humans seem universally drawn to religious ideas. This is a good book and an important book, read It soon. His web site is at http://ase.tufts.edu/cogstud/incbios/dennettd/dennettd.htm.

Durant, Will (1885 –1981)	*The Story of Philosophy* is a standard chronological reference that covers the basic ideas of the great philosophers from Plato and Socrates to the twentieth century philosophers of America and Europe.
Hitchens, Christopher	After a Cambridge/Oxford education and establishing a career as a journalist in his native England, he moved to the US where he contributes to Vanity Fair, Harpers, and other periodicals. He wrote *god is not Great: How Religion Poisons Everything* as the ultimate argument against religion. Articles by and about Hitchens can be found at http://www.hitchenszone.com/.
Frost, S. E. Jr.	Another great reference work in philosophy, *Basic Teachings of the Great Philosophers*, takes a subject approach rather than chronological, examining how major philosophers dealt with important philosophical questions or problems.
Huxley, Aldous (1894–1963)	Best known for his novels, *Brave New* World and *Island,* Huxley was a prolific author in many genres. *The Perennial Philosophy* is a classic for good reason, don't miss it; it covers a number of the aspects of the relationship between man and the Absolute. By the end of his life Huxley was considered, by some, a leader of modern thought and an intellectual of the highest rank.
Krishnamurti, Jiddu (1895–1986)	Krishnamurti was literally raised to be spiritual leader of the Order of the Star in the East, a religion that would be created for him to lead, but when he was 34 he renounced his position as its leader and dissolved the organization founded around him. He travelled the world talking to both audiences and individuals (i.e., David Bohm) about the need for a radical change in mankind. I liked *The Ending of Time*, a fascinating interaction with David Bohm. His ideas are the focus of several web sites, I liked http://www.jkrishnamurti.org/.

Loy, David	Loy is a genuine international academic, *Nonduality: A Study in Comparative Philosophy*, was written in 1988. Originally published by Yale University Press, this book covers the gamut of Eastern philosophy and explains nonduality clearly in language suited to academics.
Palmer, Donald	It's a rare reference work that can take a difficult, perhaps even painfully difficult, subject and make it fun. Fun may be a lot to ask, but Palmer has certainly justified the subtitle of *Looking at Philosophy: The Unbearable Heaviness of Philosophy Made Lighter*. This reference book takes a chronological look at twenty-five hundred years of ideas about ideas. He has taken a lighthearted approach, added drawings that are both clever and amusing, all written in a casual font. I cringe at the thought of using "fun" and "philosophy" in the same sentence, but this books tempts me.
Wilber, Ken	Wilber wrote his first book, *The Spectrum of Consciousness*, in 1977. In 1979, he wrote *No Boundary*, setting the tone for a lifetime promoting a nondual perspective. What he teaches is an integrated approach to an enlightened life combining ideas from a number of disciplines. Find more information on Ken Wilber, his books, The Integral Institute, and much more at http://www.kenwilber.com/home/landing/index.html.

Science, Metascience, and Pseudoscience

The books in this list do not necessarily endorse, accept, or even acknowledge nonduality. What they do is to present ways of looking at the world that may be unfamiliar, they are good reading, sound ideas, recommended as exercises in "mind-stretching."

Bohm, David (1917–1992)

A contemporary and colleague of Albert Einstein, Bohm was both a scientist and a philosopher. Several of the dialogues between Bohm & J. Krishnamurti were published, I have *The Ending of Time* as a book and *The Future of Humanity* as a video. I also have *Unfolding Meaning*, *Thought as a System*, and *On Creativity*. The clearest view of how his science and philosophy come together is in *Wholeness and the Implicate Order*. Bohm's implicate order is his interpretation of the unity of reality. Web site at http://www.david-bohm.net.

Braden, Gregg

Braden has become quite a prominent figure in New Age circles, with a plethora of books and videos, as well as an extensive speaking schedule. His stated mission is to unite spirituality with science. His background is in computer science and he has become an authority on ancient cultures. I have seen his video, *Awakening to Zero Point*, and read *The Divine Matrix* and his latest, *Fractal Time*. I like his writing style and I always have a good time, as I too, enjoy exploring the connections between science and spirituality. Information regarding public appearances, tours of sacred sites, books, and videos can be found at http://www.greggbraden.com/.

Capra, Fritjof

One of the first books I read relating Eastern philosophy to the new physics, *The Tao of Physics* is a New Age classic that in 1975 announced the convergence of science and spirituality in quantum physics. While maintaining a full life as a scientist and college professor Capra continues to write books that make scientific ideas more accessible to the general public. See his web site at http://www.fritjofcapra.net/.

Davis, Paul	Hard science is the watchword for this professor and researcher, and though he does not favor mysticism, science to the extreme takes us to the same end. Davis has written more than a dozen books about science for the lay audience. *The Mind of God* falls near the middle chronologically. This book is the science of reality by a real scientist; his web site is at http://cosmos.asu.edu/.
Dossey, Larry	Promoting the validity of mind based healing, in *Reinventing Medicine* Dossey, for years a practicing physician, looks at the future of medicine in areas that are now considered alternative. His focus in this book is the power of the human mind in focused mental energy, such as prayer and intention. For Dossey, the data speaks for itself, and this book has references that range from medical journals to *Reader's Digest*. His web site is at http://www.dosseydossey.com/larry/default.html.
Einstein, Albert (1879 –1955)	Explained by the man himself, *Relativity: A clear explanation that anyone can understand*, delivers the essence of these world changing theories, both special and general relativity, in 157 pages, including five appendices. Brilliant; what else can I say?
Grof, Stanislav	*Psychology of the Future* is an examination of the development and perspective of transpersonal psychology as explained by the leading expert in the field. Grof is a psychiatrist with more than fifty years experience in researching the healing and transformative potential of non-ordinary states of consciousness. Since drugs such as LSD used in early studies are now illegal, Grof has devised a system of holotropic breathwork to induce altered states of consciousness. Transpersonal psychology deals with all states of consciousness, including enlightenment. Books, audio, and video are offered for sale, and articles are available to download at http://www.stanislavgrof.com/.

Harris, Thomas A. (1910–1995)	Expanding on the Transactional Analysis of Eric Berne, *I'm OK, You're OK*, was one of the first successful "self help" books. Harris takes the ideas of superego, ego, and id from Freud and characterizes them using the more familiar terms of Parent, Adult, and Child, respectively. Depending on the situation, we communicate from one of these three positions. His premise is that meaningful and productive communication can only take place between Adults.
Hawking, Steven	Good science stuff from the most renowned physicist since Einstein, *A Brief History of Time* and *The Theory of Everything*. Both books are surprisingly easy, and enjoyable, to read. His simple web site has more info at http://www.hawking.org.uk/.
Kaufman, Steven	This theory of everything is only missing the really hard math. Kaufman's *Unified Reality Theory: the Evolution of Existence Into Experience,* tells us how the universe gets something from nothing and creates the reality we experience. Part II of the book discusses human consciousness then dives enthusiastically into nonduality, ultimately allowing everything to fall back into nothingness. The story of the book and its author, and book excerpts are at http://www.unifiedreality.com/.
Laszlo, Ervin	Laszlo is a systems philosopher, futurist, and concert pianist. He is a cofounder of the Club of Budapest, an organization promoting "a new way of thinking and a new ethics that will help resolve the social, political, economic, and ecological challenges of the 21st century." His book, *The Chaos Point* is a hard hitting look at the future based on chaos theory. It traces this shift of conscious into 2012 and beyond. A scholar of the highest order, information on this amazing man and his work is at the web sites http://www.clubofbudapest.org/index.php and http://www.worldshiftnetwork.org/home/index.html.

McTaggart, Lynne	A journalist becomes involved in the search for free energy and finds much more. *The Field: The Quest for the Secret Force of the Universe* talks about the field that underlies reality and the light that emanates from living things. She has also written *The Intention Experiment*, an ongoing investigation and data gathering project in support of the premise that intention can change reality. The web site, http://theintentionexperiment.ning.com/, offers access to current results of the experiment and the opportunity to participate.
Morris, Desmond	This British Zoologist wrote two books that relate to human behavior. In 1967 he wrote *The Naked Ape*, which drew behavioral comparisons between humans and other animals. In 1969, he published *The Human Zoo*, in which he theorized that the evolution of the human animal was not keeping pace with the culture we are creating. In his theory, people were evolved only to the point where they were suited to life in small, extended family tribes, but were captives in massive modern cities, which he likened to zoos of our own making. Ethnic enclaves, neighborhood watches, and street gangs are evidence of our tendency to form this type of smaller familiar group within the larger urban environment. At his web site, http://www.desmond-morris.com/index.php, there is information on his writings, most of which deal with animal behavior, and his work as a surrealist artist.
Talbot, Michael (1953–1992)	Talbot wrote novels as well as nonfiction. Both *The Holographic Universe* and *Mysticism and the New Physics* are good science, his easy style draws parallels between Eastern mysticism and new physics. I am not familiar with his fiction, but based on the two books that I have read, any of his nonfiction are good bets. It is a loss to the world that this brilliant man died so young.

Wade, Jenny	*Changes of Mind: A Holonomic Theory of the Evolution of Consciousness* is a detailed view of a stage theory developed by the author, a transpersonal psychologist. In her theory, there are nine stages of consciousness spanning from pre-birth to post-death, and reaching the pinnacle in the Unitive stage. This is a fascinating analysis of human consciousness and how it evolves. In her theory, Unitive Consciousness corresponds to enlightenment.
Wolf, Fred Alan	Anything by Wolf should be solid science and good entertainment mixed with lots of nonduality. In this regard, *The Dreaming Universe*, does not disappoint. Not offered as a theory of everything, it is an interesting way of looking at a reality in which all the pieces fit. Wolf (aka Dr. Quantum), is a hoot to read and makes a strong scientific case for a reality that can only stand on a foundation of nonduality. His web site, more fun, is http://www.fredalanwolf.com/.
Zukav, Gary	Since Zukav wrote *The Dancing Wu Li Masters* in 1979, he has become something of a New Age phenomenon. His second book, *Seat of the Soul,* in my opinion, was not as good as his first. Since that time he has written several more books which have been expanded into an extensive teaching role and formed The Seat of the Soul Institute. In 2007, he was on the Oprah show. His web site is at http://www.zukav.com/home.html.

Books about dealing with duality

These books, and the authors they represent, are directed to the sincere seeker who is ready to be jarred out of the mind's dualistic trance. They all address the transition from seeker to finder and do it very well. The first book by McKenna triggered an awakening for me. The others are books that I read after the awakening, which I believe might have affected me had I read them before. This is important work during these times of shifting consciousness. I reiterate that this is an incomplete list, and that authors not in this list are not necessarily inferior to or less valid than those who are included.

Ardagh, Arjuna	*The Translucent Revolution* talks about the shift of consciousness that is taking place in the world today. He emphasizes the pervasiveness of the shift and addresses it from both an individual and collective view. This is a thought provoking and well written book, and though it is kind of long at about 500 pages, it is a joy to read. Find books, audio, and video by this author and courses available at The Living Essence Foundation at http://www.livingessence.com/home.php
McKenna, Jed	After reading McKenna's first book, *Spiritual Enlightenment; The Damnedest Thing*, I wanted to find out more about the author. Not only was no information available, but rumors were out that the alleged author/protagonist and the Iowa farmhouse/ashram in the book, where he supposedly taught, were both fictional. Nevertheless, his first book marked a turning point for me and launched the writing of *Sophia*, so I gotta say I loved it. His first book was a series of vignettes centering on various interactions with and activities of one central character – Jed. Strong elements of truth and interesting stories and characters.

His second book, *Spiritually Incorrect Enlightenment*, was more complex, with non-spiritual literary references, which I found distracting, such as the persistently pursued idea that Herman Melville's Captain Ahab from *Moby Dick* represents the archetype of the spiritual seeker. I didn't care much for his second book and have not yet read his third or fourth. In both books, he has an aggressive style that is direct and potentially offensive to more delicate egos. He teaches a Zen-like path via parables and stories. You can find information about his books at http://www.wisefoolpress.com/.

Tolle, Eckhart   Tolle knows nonduality and expresses it extremely well. His teachings are a synthesis between nondual principles and dealing with the duality in which we live. Oprah ran a ten week program on the Internet as a chapter by chapter open discussion of Tolle's latest book, *A New Earth*. There are free downloads of the program available on her web site. His first big hit was *The Power of Now*, which, though it was written as Q&A, made the best of that format. His web site is at http://www.eckharttolle.com/eckharttolle, and offers books, audio, and video, as well as articles and free downloads.

Recommended traditional readings

As I have made clear throughout the book, I personally don't care for traditional teachings. I would be hard pressed to recommend spiritual texts that are the products of ancient cultures. I also have not developed much of an appreciation for poetry. Yet the two writings below, which I heartily recommend, are both recognized ancient spiritual texts, and both are written as poetry. Go figure.

Lao Tzu   *The Tao te Ching* is the primary scripture of Taoism. I have the translation by Brain Browne Walker, A short Foreword by the translator, leads, without commentary to the verse which runs only 81 pages. It is profound poetry of nonduality in its simplest expression.

Traditional   In the Hindu system, *The Ashtavakra Gita* is also written as poetry. I have a translation by Ramesh Balsekar (*A Duet of One*) with extensive commentary. I didn't care for this book as I think the AG is a very simple piece and to me needs little if any commentary. If you require expert commentary, Balsekar is one of many available. You can also find it free on the Internet and most versions print out as about twenty pages of verse.

13246060R00163